CONTENTS

WHOOPS - FORGOT MY GLOVES!

Nick Arnold has been writing stories and books since he was a youngster, but never dreamt he'd find fame writing about Chemical Chaos. His research involved being blown up, sucking helium out of balloons and cooking up revolting substances and he enjoyed every minute of it.

When he's not delving into Horrible Science, he spends his spare time teaching adults in a college. His hobbies include eating pizza, riding his bike and thinking up corny jokes (though not all at the same time).

Tony De Saulles picked up his crayons when he was still in nappies and has been doodling ever since. He takes Horrible Science very seriously and even agreed to test out some of our explosive experiments before drawing them. Fortunately, his injuries weren't too serious.

When he's not out with his sketchpad, Tony likes to write poetry and play squash, though he hasn't written any poetry about squash yet.

HORRIBLE SCIENCE

CHEMICAL CHAOS

NICK ARNOLD

illustrated by
TONY DE SAULLES

SCHOLASTIC

Scholastic Children's Books,
Euston House, 24 Eversholt Street,
London, NW1 1DB, UK

A division of Scholastic Ltd
London ~ New York ~ Toronto ~ Sydney ~ Auckland
Mexico City ~ New Delhi ~ Hong Kong

First published in the UK by Scholastic Ltd, 1997
This edition published 2008

Text copyright © Nick Arnold, 1997
Illustrations © Tony De Saulles, 1997

ISBN 978 0439 94450 2

Printed in the UK by CPI Bookmarque, Croydon

13 15 17 19 20 18 16 14

The right of Nick Arnold and Tony De Saulles to be identified as the author and
illustrator of this work respectively has been asserted by them in accordance with
the Copyright, Designs and Patents Act, 1988.

INTRODUCTION

Chemistry can be summed up in a single word – "UGH!".
It's that part of science to do with chemicals and test tubes.
"Ugh!" is the best word for it! It's the most *horrible* part
of Horrible Science.

And why is it so horrible? Well – if you find science
confusing you'll find chemistry as clear as mud. It can
cause chaos in your brain.

For starters, there are those chaotic-sounding chemical
names. Like poly methyl metha crylate* (say polly me-
thile-me-tha-cry-late). *That's the acrylic in your jumper,
if you didn't already know.

THAT'S AN ATTRACTIVE
POLYACRYLONITRITE
GARMENT YOU'RE WEARING!*

*TRANSLATION – I LIKE YOUR ACRYLIC JUMPER

These long words are mainly Latin or Greek. Fine for
ancient Romans – but horribly confusing for the rest of
us. Sometimes chemistry turns totally chaotic. That's
when chemists talk their own chaotic code language.

THIS H_2O HASN'T YET
REACHED 100°

I REQUIRE SOME
$C_{12}H_{22}O_{11}$

THIS LACTIC ACID
SMELLS UNPLEASANT

TRANSLATION:
1 The water hasn't boiled.
2 Pass the sugar.
3 Lactic acid = sour milk: the milk's gorn orf!

Even a chemist's brain seems pretty chaotic. How else would they come to investigate soggy cornflakes? (Chemists have reported that a cornflake with more than 18 per cent milk content is just too soggy to study.)

But funnily enough that's what this book is about. Not the bits you learn in school – but the funny bits and the fascinating bits, the bits you really want to find out about … nasty bubbling green mixtures, vile and sometimes poisonous potions, test tubes, horrible smells, bangs, blasts and dodgy discoveries.

And who knows, *Chemical Chaos* might just help you see through the confusion that is chemistry. Then you might just end up causing chaos in your chemistry teacher's day, by getting your own experiments to work…

CHAOTIC CHEMISTS

Chemists are curiously chaotic. Their knowledge of chemicals used to be chaotically confused and their messed-up experiments caused chaos too. The first chemists were called alchemists and they were pretty chaotic. And strange.

Imagine it's a particularly boring chemistry lesson, and you are feeling ver-r-ry sleepy. The next thing you know you are in a mysterious room... You see an old man reading a book. He is surrounded by oddly-shaped flasks, the stumps of candles and dirty beakers. On a nearby table there are bottles of ink, tatty goose feather pens, oily rags and old musty books – full of ancient dust and secrets. In the chaotic shadows stand row upon row of bottles filled with weird potions. On the floor lie the rat-nibbled remains of several meals. The old man laughs to himself. Then in a thin crackly voice he reads a magical spell...

EYE OF NEWT,
WING OF BAT,
FOOTBALL BOOT,
TAIL OF CAT!

Confused? Don't worry this is NOT your chemistry teacher! You've just slipped back 500 years to meet your local chemist. Except 500 years ago chemists weren't called chemists – they were called alchemists.

A note to the reader

> Dear reader, as far as this book is concerned a chemist is NOT a shop where you buy pills. A chemist is someone who studies chemicals. O.K.?

APPALLING ALCHEMISTS

As far as we know, alchemy started in Ancient Greece and China. It's a mixture of chemical knowledge, magic and philosophy about how materials are formed. On a more practical level, alchemists tried to turn cheap metals into gold. Here's one of their more unusual recipes.

YE OLD ALCHEMIST'S RECIPE FOR MAKING GOLD.

1. Take some alum (that's a compound of aluminium, sulphur, potassium and oxygen).

2. Add some coal dust, pyrites (iron ore) and a few drops of mercury (the runny metal found in thermometers).

3. Mix well.

4. Stir in an ounce of cinnamon (spicy-tasting tree-bark) and half a dozen egg yolks. Keep stirring until the mixture is gooey.

5. Then add a generous dollop of fresh horse dung. Keep stirring.

6. Finally, add some sal ammoniac. (This is a poisonous mixture of ammonia and chlorine found in volcanoes.)

7. Bake well in a hot oven for six hours. The result should be pure gold. If you're lucky.

A note to the reader:

Dear reader, don't bother trying this for yourself. It doesn't work – honest!

Although some people poked fun at its more curious notions – alchemy was fashionable. Even kings wanted to try it. It has been suggested that the British King Charles II was poisoned by the mercury he used for alchemy experiments. His scientist pal Sir Isaac Newton used this substance for experiments and it's said he went mad for two years.

Bet you never knew!
One famous alchemist was the Arab writer Geber (or Jeber). Now old Geb had lots of ideas but he was a lousy writer. In fact, his boring books of experiments gave rise to the word "gibberish". Sadly, Geber wasn't the last scientist to come out with a load of old gibberish.

Here's another alchemist's trick you shouldn't try.

TO WARM A LIQUID

Surround a jar of the liquid with horse manure. Germs in the dung cause chemical reactions which produce heat. This really works – but if you do want to keep your tea warm try a thermos flask – it's less smelly!

GET-RICH RUTHERFORD?

Despite many failures the alchemists kept going. They believed a substance called the "philosopher's stone" would turn cheap metals into gold. No one knew what the philosopher's stone was exactly or where to find it. But alchemists were convinced that the person who found the stone would live for ever. Of course, no one ever discovered the real answer. Until quite recently...

In 1911 New Zealander Ernest Rutherford (1871–1937) found out how to change metals into gold. This involved the metals' atoms, which are the minuscule objects that make up all substances. To make the gold, you zap bits off the atoms with a high-energy ray. By changing the atoms you can change the metal they form.

But Rutherford had bad news for alchemists:

1 Atoms are so tiny they're easy to miss with your zapping ray.

2 The easiest metal to turn into gold is platinum. But that's even more expensive than gold!

3 So if you want gold it really is cheaper to buy some from your local jeweller!

CHAOTIC CHEMISTS OF THE PAST

By 1700 scientists were becoming curious about chemicals for reasons other than alchemy. They dropped the "al" bit as well, and called themselves "chemists" instead. "Al" only means "the" in Arabic anyway. But many people thought chemistry was a strange idea. One scientist, Justus von Liebig (1803–1873) was told off at school for not doing homework. His teacher asked him what job he wanted to do and Justus said he wanted to be a chemist whereupon...

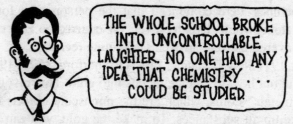

THE WHOLE SCHOOL BROKE INTO UNCONTROLLABLE LAUGHTER. NO ONE HAD ANY IDEA THAT CHEMISTRY ... COULD BE STUDIED.

One man played a vital role in begining to change their minds. His name was Antoine Lavoisier (1743–1794). Some people even called him the "Father of Modern Chemistry". But in 1789 revolution swept France and Lavoisier found himself in a seriously chaotic situation.

AN ENEMY OF THE PEOPLE?

It was a time of terror but no one dared use the word. No one was safe from arrest. In the Square of the Revolution there were daily executions for the old women to watch as they sat knitting in the spring sunshine.

MERCY!

WHY DO THEY ALWAYS SAY "THANKYOU"?

"Pass me ze papers," said the Public Prosecutor to his newly-appointed clerk. "Yes, the ones about Citizen Lavoisier."

The young man hurriedly searched his desk. It was unwise to waste the Prosecutor's time. The Prosecutor, Antoine Fouquier-Tinville, was always in a hurry.

"*Merci* – thank you," said the Prosecutor, and he hastily examined the paper. "Aha, Antoine Lavoisier – the collector of taxes…"

"He's a great scientist too…" ventured the clerk.

"WHO dares say so!" screamed the Prosecutor.

The clerk dropped his quill pen and papers in a shower of ink. "I mean, I didn't mean that!" he stammered. "I meant Lavoisier is a great traitor! Oh, silly me!"

"Well," said the Prosecutor, "let's see what the file says." He began reading the document in the harsh voice he used to terrify prisoners in court:

"Antoine Lavoisier. Born 1743 and brought up by his aunt, father and grandmother… Hmm – he was a swot at school. Spent one year in which his only lessons were science and maths. Pah! Two more years learning nothing but philosophy. Pah! Pah! Wrote his first scientific paper at the age of ten – what a little creep! Later found gypsum has water in it and mineral water has tiny bits of salt. Very useful … I *don't* think. Ha, ha!"

"I … I know," said the clerk from the floor in a small

13

voice, "that Lavoisier is a traitor … but … he did find that water contains hydrogen and oxygen chemicals. Then he discovered gases in the air. Then he found you can't destroy chemicals – only change them around and then…"

"Stop, you fool!" spat the Prosecutor. "Do you think I need ze chemistry lesson?! Ah – here's the juicy bit. In 1768 Citizen Lavoisier became a tax collector. One of his friends said, 'The dinners he will give us will be so much the better!' All the *tax* collectors are the enemies of the people. Thanks to the revolution they're in prison now!"

The Prosecutor smiled unpleasantly. "Let's see if they enjoy their fine dinners without their heads on!" He drew his finger across his throat and made a choking sound.

"Excuse me – I've got some papers to file!" said the clerk as he fled the room in panic. He just missed a thin man in a green coat. The visitor was plainly dressed apart from his white powdered hair. He certainly didn't look like the most powerful man in France. But that's who he was.

"Citizen Robespierre," said the Public Prosecutor with a false smile. "This is indeed a pleasure and an honour. The papers await your signature."

"More enemies of the people?" enquired Robespierre. He seated himself without being asked and read the document. "Lavoisier. Yes, I remember him. He supported the revolution at first. Helped with the new metric weights too. He did good work for France running gunpowder factories before the revolution. He would be a great loss."

The Prosecutor frowned. He was unsure if Robespierre was testing his loyalty and replied nervously, "Our revolutionary hero, Citizen Marat, called Lavoisier a traitor in his newspaper articles."

"Yes, I know," said Robespierre. "But Marat was a failed scientist and Lavoisier was rude enough to say so. That's why Marat hated him so much."

"So. You mean us to spare Citizen Lavoisier?"

Robespierre merely smiled coldly and gazed out of the window. The pen was poised like a dagger in his hand.

Antoine Lavoisier's trial began on 8 May, 1794. The scientist looked pale and tired after six months in prison. He pleaded for more time to finish a vital chemistry experiment. Would Robespierre take pity on him? What do *you* think the verdict was?

a) GUILTY. The Judge said, "The Republic has no need for scientists." and Lavoisier was beheaded that afternoon.

b) NOT GUILTY. The Judge said, "The Republic should spare the life of such a great scientist."

c) GUILTY. The Judge said, "But we'll give you a month to finish off your experiment."

Answer: a) One of Lavoisier's friends said, "It took them only an instant to cut off that head, and another hundred years may not produce another like it." Two months later Robespierre lost power and was put to death. Fouquier-Tinville was executed the following year. And Lavoisier's work lives on…

CHAOTIC CONTEMPORARY CHEMISTS

Nowadays, there are thousands of chemists. In the USA alone there are over 140,000 chemists trying to discover new chemicals! Some are looking for ultra-light metals or new kinds of plastics. Others are looking for new food ingredients or medical drugs. Here's where they work.

A CHEMISTRY LAB

At first sight all these bits and pieces look a bit funny. But they all have their uses.

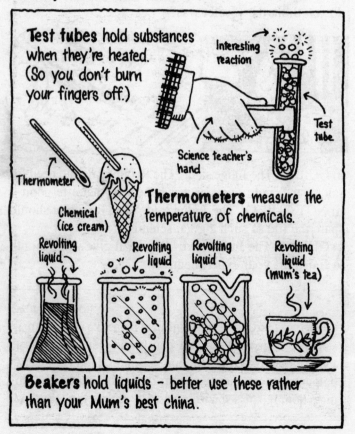

Test tubes hold substances when they're heated. (So you don't burn your fingers off.)

Interesting reaction

Test tube

Science teacher's hand

Thermometer

Chemical (ice cream)

Thermometers measure the temperature of chemicals.

Revolting liquid

Revolting liquid

Revolting liquid

Revolting liquid (mum's tea)

Beakers hold liquids – better use these rather than your Mum's best china.

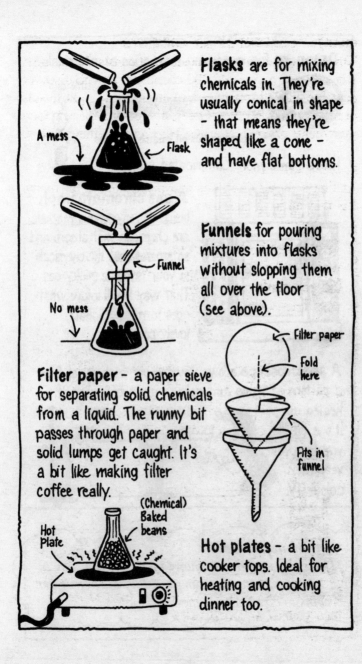

Flasks are for mixing chemicals in. They're usually conical in shape – that means they're shaped like a cone – and have flat bottoms.

A mess

Flask

Funnels for pouring mixtures into flasks without slopping them all over the floor (see above).

Funnel

No mess

Filter paper

Fold here

Fits in funnel

Filter paper – a paper sieve for separating solid chemicals from a liquid. The runny bit passes through paper and solid lumps get caught. It's a bit like making filter coffee really.

(Chemical) Baked beans

Hot Plate

Hot plates – a bit like cooker tops. Ideal for heating and cooking dinner too.

Droppers for measuring little drips of chemicals.

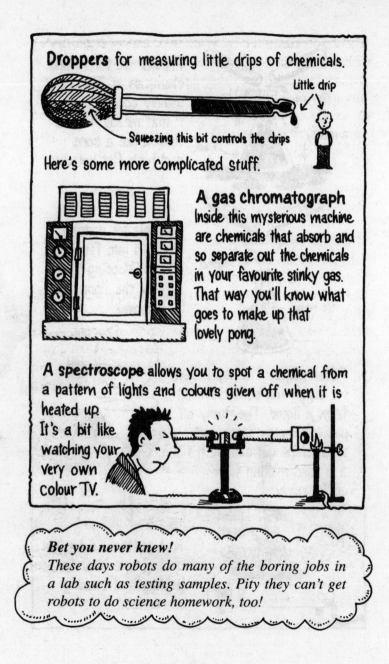

Little drip

Squeezing this bit controls the drips

Here's some more complicated stuff.

A gas chromatograph
Inside this mysterious machine are chemicals that absorb and so separate out the chemicals in your favourite stinky gas. That way you'll know what goes to make up that lovely pong.

A spectroscope allows you to spot a chemical from a pattern of lights and colours given off when it is heated up. It's a bit like watching your very own colour TV.

Bet you never knew!
These days robots do many of the boring jobs in a lab such as testing samples. Pity they can't get robots to do science homework, too!

Dare you discover … your own secret substance?

If being a chemist sounds like fun here's your chance to make a laughably easy discovery.

You will need:

2 teaspoonfuls of cream of tartar (available from supermarkets)

1 cup of salt

2 cups of plain flour

2 cups of water

2 tablespoonfuls of cooking oil

What you do:

1 Mix the flour and salt in a large saucepan.

2 Add the water and mix well.

3 Add the cream of tartar and the cooking oil and mix well.

4 Ask an adult to help you heat the saucepan on a low heat and stir it until the mixture thickens. Leave to cool.

Like any other inventor you'll need to find a use for your new discovery. That's up to you – here's a few daft ideas.

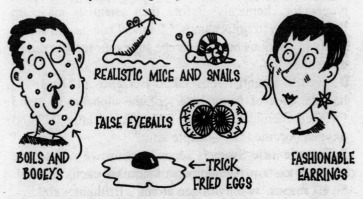

REALISTIC MICE AND SNAILS

FALSE EYEBALLS

BOILS AND BOGEYS

←TRICK FRIED EGGS

FASHIONABLE EARRINGS

Finally, you'll need to dream up a name for your new substance … any suggestions?

CHAOTIC CHEMICAL EXPRESSIONS

Were chemists just having a laugh when they thought up names like polyvinylidenechloride? What do you think they were talking about?

WHAT'S IN A NAME?

So, how do scientists decide on a name for all these new substances? And do they have to be so long and complicated?

1 In 1787 Lavoisier suggested that scientists should agree names for chemicals. Before then scientists made up their own mysterious names. Chemical names still sound pretty mysterious but you can be sure your teacher didn't make them up.

2 Swedish scientist Jöns Jakob Berzelius (1779–1848) had the idea of using letters of the alphabet to stand for each chemical atom. So hydrogen became "H" and oxygen became "O" – simple innit?

3 The scientific Swede's second brainwave was to use numbers to show the numbers of atoms in each chemical. So H_2 means "two hydrogen atoms". Brilliant – eh?

4 When you get two or more atoms joined together it's called a molecule. $2H_2$ means two lots of two hydrogen atoms and H_2O is a molecule of the two hydrogen atoms and an oxygen atom joined together.

5 In fact H_2O is just the chemists' code for plain boring old water.

But anyone can be a chemist. In fact, you may be one without even realizing it. And if that sounds incredible – consider this: you use chemistry every time you cook or wash up. Shocking, isn't it?

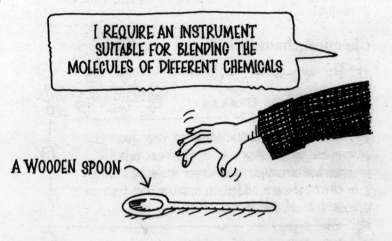

I REQUIRE AN INSTRUMENT SUITABLE FOR BLENDING THE MOLECULES OF DIFFERENT CHEMICALS

A WOODEN SPOON

CHAOTIC KITCHEN CHEMISTRY

How can cookery possibly be chemical? Actually, it would be impossible to cook without chemistry. It's what cooking's all about – from the suspect substances that call themselves school dinners, to the revolting reaction that makes your dad's homemade rice pudding stick to its dish.

Chemical chaos fact file

Name: Food chemicals

The basic facts: Most of your food is made up of atoms of a chemical called carbon arranged into larger molecules. Other chemicals are added to improve the taste or texture of the food.

Horrible details: In the nineteenth century mysterious things were added to food to make it go further. For example, ground-up bones were mixed into flour. And wooden strawberry pips were added to "strawberry" jam to make it look more real!

I WISH YOU HADN'T TOLD ME THAT

KITCHEN CHEMISTRY LAB

It's a strange thought, but your kitchen is a bit like a chemistry lab.

THE SOUP HASN'T REACHED THE OPTIMUM TEMPERATURE YET

CONCAVE COMBINATION UTENSIL (BOWL)

HEAT ENERGY CONDUCTOR (COOKER)

METALLIC CHEMICAL COMPOUNDER (SPOON)

SPOUTED RECEPTACLE (JUG)

METALLIC SMALL SOLIDS MANIPULATOR (TONGS)

Some machines in your kitchen are mysteriously similar to instruments used by scientists.

PRESSURE COOKER

This works by allowing water to boil at a higher temperature than usual, so it cooks things faster. But it's similar to a machine called an autoclave that kills germs on scientific instruments.

THERMOS FLASK

This is handy for keeping your soup hot or a drink cold on a summer's day. But the flask was originally invented by a chemist. In 1892 Sir James Dewar invented the double-walled container to keep his chemicals cold.

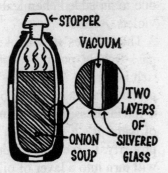

←STOPPER

VACUUM

TWO LAYERS OF SILVERED GLASS

ONION SOUP

COOKER

This is simply a machine for heating food chemicals to produce the chemical reactions that we call cooking.

WHAT'S THAT SMELL, MUM?

Here are some fascinating food facts to impress your friends during school lunchbreak. (You'll impress them even more if you can work out what you're eating.)

SIX MIXED-UP FOOD FACTS

1 The burning sensation you get if you eat chilli peppers is due to a chemical called capsaicin (cap-say-kin). According to experts the best remedy for a fiery mouth is a generous helping of ice cream! That's tragic!

SWEAT

HOT GLOW

2 The smell of raspberries found in most yoghurts is due to an added chemical called ionone. It's made from violets. Aah!

3 The bubbles in a cooked cake mixture are made by gas! Baking powder contains an acid and a chemical rich in carbon. When they're heated, a chemical reaction produces a gas called carbon dioxide.

4 Salad dressing is an emulsion. No, that's not a type of paint. It's a mixture of two chemicals that don't mix properly. Leave a salad dressing for a few hours and it will turn into a layer of oil above a layer of vinegar.

24

5 Vinegar is made from wine that has gone disgustingly sour. This chemical reaction is caused by the waste products produced by germs. Yuck!

6 Toast is bread in which the carbon has been partly burnt. The smoke that sometimes pours from the toaster is made from tiny bits of carbon.

Teacher's tea-break teaser

If you are very brave (or foolhardy) knock on the door of the staffroom and try this question on your teacher.

Answer: It does make a difference. Milk contains a chemical called casein (case-in). When tea mixes with milk, chemicals called tannins in the tea can break down the casein into smaller molecules. If you add the milk to the tea it means that more casein gets broken down. This makes the tea taste of boiled milk. That's why chemists in the know add tea to milk and not the other way around!

AMAZING CHANGES

Like tea-making, cooking is about heating chemicals until they change in some way. For example, chips cook at 190°C (374°F) and meringues need several hours at 70°C (158°F). But what causes these dramatic changes?

Try these terrible trick questions on your unsuspecting cookery teacher!

1 When you are trying to boil milk why does it suddenly go "whoosh" and try to leap out of the pan?

2 The boiling point of cooking oil is hotter than the temperature needed to melt a frying pan. So how can you fry food?

Answers: 1 The milk contains fat globules that form a layer on the top of the liquid as it heats. At about 100°C the milk under the fat layer is a frenzy of boiling bubbles. Suddenly the fat layer splits allowing the milk to whoosh! **2** The food contains water that boils at its usual temperature. This boiling water cooks the food and the oil doesn't boil at all.

FOUL FERTILIZERS

Even your vegetables are not free from the mysterious activities of the chemical industry. There's a whole array of herbicides, insecticides, fungicides and pesticides sprayed on the growing plants to deter ugly bugs and weeds. Then there are *fertilizers* to make crops grow.

HOW DARE YOU! I WOULDN'T TOUCH THE STUFF!

BLUSH

FE

Phosphorous may be poisonous for humans but it's good for making fertilizer chemicals called phosphates. One traditional type of naturally phosphate-rich fertilizer is guano. It's found several metres deep on islands off the coast of Peru. And the origin of this special substance … do you really want to know? Old seabird droppings full of digested fish bones. Oh yes – bones are rich in phosphates and ground-up bones are ideal for growing plants.

Nowadays fertilizers are made by mixing sulphuric acid with phosphates found in rocks. But the chemists have not just stuck to fertilizers. Some *foods* were practically invented in a test tube.

A SLIPPERY STORY - MARGARINE

French Emperor Napoleon III organized a competition to invent a cheap butter-substitute for poor people.

Scientist Hippolyte Mége-Mouriez reckoned that anything a cow could do HE could do better.

In 1869 he came up with his magic marg ingredients:

INGREDIENTS
beef fat
skimmed milk
ice
pigs' stomach juices

UGH!

METHOD

1 Simply heat the beef fat to the body temperature of a cow.
2 Gradually pour in pigs' stomach juices.
3 Stir in the water and milk.
4 Now churn the ingredients together in a handy barrel.
5 Add ice to cool the mixture.
6 Squelch it all together.

Mouriez hoped to get rich and he opened a factory to make margarine. Unfortunately, war broke out between France and Prussia and his factory had to close down.

Two years later the idea was bought by a couple of Dutch merchants. Soon they were churning out margarine and profits.

In 1910 a shortage of animal fat led to the use of vegetable oils or smelly fish oil.

LOOKING AT THE INGREDIENTS

Most foods you can buy in a supermarket have the ingredients on the side. Some sound a bit weird. Margarine, for example usually contains…

• hydrogenated oils
• emulsifier
• antioxidants
• vitamins
• water

Emulsifiers are chemicals with two ends. One likes oils and one likes water. So this marvellous molecule cleverly joins the water and the oil molecules together.

Antioxidants stop the margarine going off, or rancid. Sage and rosemary plants include natural antioxidants often used by food manufacturers.

Hydrogenation means adding hydrogen molecules to the margarine. This makes the marg harder and more like butter.

Vitamins are a group of different chemicals you can get from different foods. Vitamins keep your body healthy. Margarine doesn't contain some vitamins so they are added to make it healthier to eat.

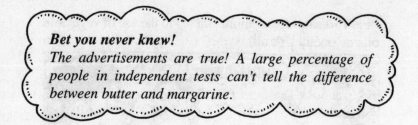
CHAOTIC CHEMICAL COOKERY

Besides margarine, lots of chemists have made food from chemicals you definitely wouldn't want to eat.

1 Alexander Butlerov (1828–1886) found that formaldehyde (for-mal-de-hide) can be treated to make a type of sugar called glucose. Formaldehyde is a horrible smelly chemical used to preserve bits of dead body.

2 During the Second World War German chemists discovered how to make fat from oil – not cooking oils but the sort of oil you put in a car! Mmm, tasty!

Dare you discover ... some chemical cookery?

Try creating a little bit of chemical chaos in your kitchen with these experimental recipes.

1 *Yucky yeast* Yeast is no mere chemical. It's ALIVE! Yes – yeast is a tiny fungus like the mould that grows on stale bread. Ugh! Yeast is harmless but its horrible relatives can cause skin infections and some diseases of the lungs and guts.

You will need:
Some dried yeast (you can get packets from supermarkets)
Teaspoon and tablespoon for mixing
A small bowl and glass
Sugar
Warm water

What you do:
1 Mix a sachet (that's 7 grams) of yeast with a small glassful of warm water.
2 Stir in a teaspoonful of sugar until it dissolves.
3 Leave the bowl in a warm place for an hour and check what's happened.

a) The mixture has turned bright red.
b) The liquid froths up and has a funny smell.
c) Small crystals have formed in the mixture and it stinks.

Answer: b) The yeast eats up the sugar and produces alcohol and carbon dioxide – that's the froth. This is also what happens when people make wine from grape juice.

2 *Terrific toffee* Sugar is a complicated compound (mixture) of chemicals including carbon, hydrogen and oxygen atoms. Many sweets are simply sugar that's been heated to a particular temperature. For example, fudge is made at 116°C (241°F), caramel at 120°C (248°F) and the hottest of all … toffee. Here's how to make it.

You will need:
An adult to help you
25 g butter
100 g castor sugar
7.5 ml water
A sugar thermometer
A tablespoon and saucepan
A bowl of ice-cold water
Some chopped apple with skin attached
Enough cocktail sticks for every bit of apple

What you do:
1 Stick a cocktail stick in each of the chopped apple pieces.
2 Mix the sugar, water and butter in the saucepan.
3 Heat the mixture to 160°C (320°F). Stir it gently. Notice how the sugar turns into a brown, melted, gungey mass on the way.
4 Dip some apple in the mixture. Be careful – it's very hot! Then dip the apple into the cold water for about 20 seconds to cool it down.
5 Eat it!

And after that there's nothing else for it – you've got to wash up. It's a mystery where half the washing-up comes from. Never mind, even the really great scientists had to do this. And luckily, there's lots of chemical cleaners to help you!

SQUEAKY CLEANERS

There's bound to be a few squeaks of protest when it comes to washing greasy dishes or getting soggy in a boring old bath. But it's got to be done, so where would we be without cleaning chemicals? Somewhere disgustingly dirty – that's where!

Chemical chaos fact file

Name: Soap

The basic facts: Soap is a salt made from acids and alkalis taken from fats. Soap is the layer you skim off the top of the mixture.

Horrible details: The Romans washed in soap to treat elephantiasis, a truly disgusting disease in which tiny worms get under the skin. The soap was useless as a cure.

IT'S NOT WORKING

A SOAP OPERA

1 The first soap was mixed-up fat and wood ash. It was probably invented when someone's cookery went chaotically wrong.

2 Soap was used in France about 2,000 years ago by an ancient people called the Gauls. They claimed that soap made from goat fat kept their hair nice and shiny.

3 Eighteenth-century soap was made by mixing boiling fat and soda. The soda rips the fat molecules apart and soap results. Mind you, too much soda dissolves your skin! Nasty.

4 Luckily, before 1853 soap was so heavily taxed that many people couldn't afford to use it.

5 In 1900 people washed clothes using soap. (Washing powder hadn't been invented then.) The soap turned clothes yellow, so clothes were then dyed blue. This had the effect of making them appear white again.

6 Between 1911 and 1980 British people doubled the amount of soap they used each year. Did that mean twice as many baths?

SUPER SOAP

Soap is great for washing things because of the shape of the soap molecule. It has a long tail that sticks to dirt and a head end that's attracted to water molecules by an electrical force. The result? The soap molecule yanks the dirt into the water. Then you can wash the dirt away.

Dare you discover … a slippery soap experiment?

You will need:

Two mirrors
A bathroom
Soap

What you do:

1 Rub one mirror with a thin layer of soap.
2 Run the hot tap. Only one of the mirrors steams up.
Which one is it … and why?

a) The soapy mirror steams up because soap attracts the water in the steam.

b) The soapy mirror doesn't steam up or get wet because the soap stops the water getting to the glass.

c) The soapy mirror gets wet but doesn't steam up. The soap stops the water in the steam forming droplets on the glass.

Answer: c)

DETERGENT - WHAT'S IN IT FOR YOU?

The first detergents were developed by the Germans during the First World War. They were made from soap powders and salt. During that war the Germans had a smelly problem owing to a shortage of soap, so they used detergents instead. But these were useless – you had to rub really hard before you got any froth. But as luck would have it – the new detergent worked wonders on their woollies!

EATING UP THE DIRT

It's amazing what they fit in a box of washing powder. For example, "biological" washing powders include enzymes. These are chemicals often found in living creatures that speed up reactions between other chemicals. Washing powder enzymes help to gobble up nasty stains such as blood and egg and disgusting little bits of food. The enzyme molecules stay the same.

ACTION-PACKED POWDERS

Here are some other things you'll find in a packet of washing powder.

Builders – these are nothing to do with construction workers! These are chemicals that remove dirt and stop it sticking to anything else in the wash.

Anti-rusting chemicals stop rust from eating away your washing machine's vital innards.

Conditioners stop the grains of powder sticking together and help them to dissolve in the washing water.

Optical brighteners are chemicals that soak up ordinary light and reflect back bluish light. This makes your undies appear whiter than white. Just a clever chemical trick, really.

Dirt-bouncers are other chemicals that give dirt a tiny electrical force, making it bounce off your washing.

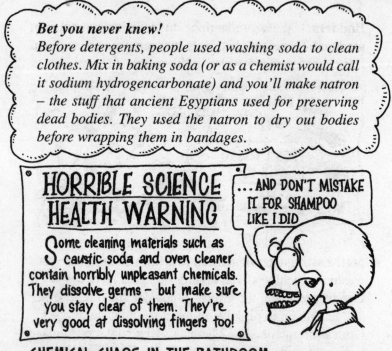

Bet you never knew!

Before detergents, people used washing soda to clean clothes. Mix in baking soda (or as a chemist would call it sodium hydrogencarbonate) and you'll make natron – the stuff that ancient Egyptians used for preserving dead bodies. They used the natron to dry out bodies before wrapping them in bandages.

HORRIBLE SCIENCE HEALTH WARNING

Some cleaning materials such as caustic soda and oven cleaner contain horribly unpleasant chemicals. They dissolve germs – but make sure you stay clear of them. They're very good at dissolving fingers too!

...AND DON'T MISTAKE IT FOR SHAMPOO LIKE I DID

CHEMICAL CHAOS IN THE BATHROOM

Your bathroom is brimming with amazing chemicals.

1 The water in your taps contains salts. It also contains calcium and magnesium salts dissolved from rocks in the ground.

2 If there is a lot of calcium and magnesium in the water it is called "hard water" and forms a revolting scum when you try to lather soap.

3 Boiling hard water changes the dissolved chemicals into chemicals that won't dissolve. That's how you get a disgusting deposit of limescale. Limescale is actually calcium carbonate – the same chemical found in chalk. You may find it lurking inside electric kettles too.

4 The first toilet cleaners were made from explosives! They were invented in 1919 when heating engineer

Harry Pickup was removing explosive waste from an ammunition factory. He dropped some in a toilet and found that the substance – nitrecake – is brilliant at cleaning. Flushed with his success, Harry opened a factory and soon became rich.

5 Talcum powder comes from volcanoes. Yes – it's true. Talc is a chemical called magnesium silicate. It's found in rocks that have been chemically changed by underground heat.

6 Toothpastes sometimes contain pumice which is another rock produced by volcanoes. (You may find pumice lurking in your bathroom anyway. It's used for scrubbing away at hard skin.)

7 Toothpaste is designed to brush away germs and stray bits of food. The first toothpastes were made from gritty substances such as chalk and jeweller's polish. They certainly wore away those nasty little stains – but they wore away people's teeth too!

Dare you discover … how to make your own toothpaste?

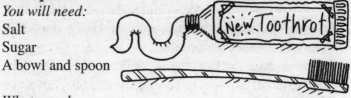

You will need:
Salt
Sugar
A bowl and spoon

What you do:
1 Mix the salt and sugar with a little water to make a paste.
2 Try it on your teeth.

Note: These ingredients really were used in the nineteenth century to make toothpaste. But don't you try them more than once. The sugar's not good for your teeth. In fact, you'd better use some proper toothpaste to remove your home-made version! Some experiments should never be repeated.

Toothpaste is just one of a huge array of strange but useful substances dreamt up by chemists. Funnily enough, chemical chaos often led to some amazing accidental discoveries.

DODGY DISCOVERIES

A chaotic combination of muddles, mishaps and mix-ups – that's how many a vital substance has been discovered. Scientists have to keep their minds open to anything that might happen during an experiment, but sometimes they might set out to answer one question, and end up solving another.

CHAOTIC CHEMISTS' COMMENTS...

Here's how some chaotic chemists describe their discoveries. Test them out on your science teacher.

"No great discovery is ever made without a bold guess."

Sir Isaac Newton (1642-1727) discoverer of gravity and big fan of alchemy.

"Failure is the mother of success."

Hideki Yukawa (1907-1981) who discovered what some of the tiny bits of atoms are made of.

"The most important of my discoveries have been suggested by my failures."

Sir Humphry Davy (1778-1829) discoverer of many new chemicals.

Many surprising substances all owe their discovery to happy accidents.

EIGHT DODGY DISCOVERIES

1 Teflon, the stuff used to coat non-stick pans was only used for this purpose after 1955 because the inventor's wife was a bad cook. She kept getting her food stuck to the bottom of the saucepan.

2 *Tracing paper* was invented by mistake in the 1930s because a worker at a paper factory put too much starch in a vat of wood pulp. The result was strong but see-though paper.

3 *Paper tissues* were designed as a new kind of make-up remover. In 1924, they were sold as disposable handkerchiefs after people wrote in saying the pads were ideal for blowing their noses.

4 *Vulcanized rubber* Early rubber boots melted in hot weather. But in 1839 Charles Goodyear spilt some boiling rubber and sulphur. He found that the resulting sticky mess didn't melt so easily.

5 *Silly Putty* the bouncy modelling clay, was discovered in 1943 when scientists attempted to make artificial rubber from silicon. The substance was no good for tyres but the chemists had a lot of fun playing with it. A sharp-eyed salesman spotted the opportunity to develop a new toy and sold 250,000 Silly Putty balls in three days.

6 *Lubricating oil* was first sold in 1690 as a cure for the painful joint disease rheumatism. The chaotic idea was that if it makes hinges move easily then it could do the same for the joints!

7 Leo Baekeland (1863–1944) discovered a new plastic through a chaotic accident. He made some fascinating chemical blobs by mixing phenol and formaldehyde. The blobs were a new kind of plastic – Bakelite. Mind you, legend has it he made the same discovery by spilling formaldehyde on his cheese sandwich!

8 *Dyes* made from chemicals in coal were discovered accidentally in 1856 by a young whiz-kid – William Perkin (1837–1907).

A colourful character

1. When Perkin was twelve a friend showed him some chemistry experiments.

THE POSSIBILITY OF NEW DISCOVERIES IMPRESSED ME VERY MUCH.

2. Young William decided to try a few chemistry experiments and a few years later enrolled in the Royal College of Science.

ROYA OF SC

REVOLTING BLACK SLUDGE
↓

3. One Easter holiday he was doing chemistry homework in his dad's garden shed. He was trying to make the medical drug, quinine, using a coal tar chemical as raw material. The result was a revolting black sludge.

4. Many scientists would have given up at this point but Perkin was intrigued. So he added alcohol, and some lovely purple crystals appeared.

5. This type of purple was a brand new colour. Nothing like it had ever been seen before. So Perkin tried making the crystals into a dye. They turned out to be ideal for dying silk.

6. Perkin sent a sample of dyed silk to a Scottish firm and received a letter in return.

Dear William

If your discovery does not make the goods too expensive, it is decidedly one of the most valuable that has come out for a long time.

Yours faithfully,
Pillars of Perth

CRIKEY!

What could be more encouraging?
7. Young William talked his dad into putting up the money for a factory to make the purple dye he called "mauvine".

8. Mauve turned out to be popular and fashionable. Soon everyone wanted to wear it. It was even used for stamps.

9. William became so rich that he was able to retire at the ripe old age of 35. He built a new house complete with private lab.

10. In 1869 he invented a red dye but a German scientist had beaten him to this discovery by one day!

11. In 1906 a celebration was held to commemorate the discovery of mauve. It was attended by the world's most distinguished scientists and business tycoons. And the guest of honour was 68-year-old William Perkin.

12. Sadly Perkin died soon afterwards. The excitement had been too much for him!

Meanwhile scientists were experimenting with plastics to find more man-made substances. And making more discoveries . . . by accident.

Chemical chaos fact file

Name: Plastic

The basic facts: Plastics are long chains of molecules based on carbon atoms. They're often made from chemicals found in petrol, but some come from coal, natural gas, cotton or even wood. Plastics are strong but bendy because the molecules are tangled up.

Horrible details: Nowadays some plastics are designed to rot in soil. They are made from carbon-dioxide and water inside microscopic germs. The plastic is removed and the germs are boiled away!

PETE'S PLASTIC COFFINS "THEY'RE ONLY £2, AND THEY ROT UNDERGROUND!"

FANTASTIC PLASTICS QUIZ

It's amazing the sheer variety of things that can be made from plastics. Which of these items do you think are made from plastics, and which sound too comical to be true?

1. DRUMHEADS

2. BOOK COVERS

3. DRINK CARTONS

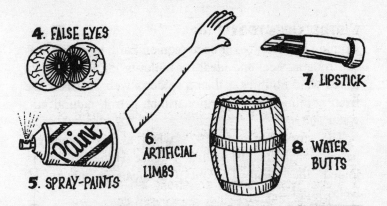

4. FALSE EYES

7. LIPSTICK

5. SPRAY-PAINTS

6. ARTIFICIAL LIMBS

8. WATER BUTTS

CHAOTIC CHEMICAL EXPRESSIONS

A chemist tells his best friend: My underwear is made from polyhexamethylene adipamide (polly-hexa-meeth-ile-ne-adi-pam-ide).

Is this dangerous?

Answer: No – he's got nylon underpants.

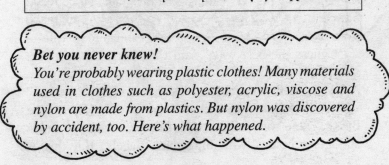

Bet you never knew!
You're probably wearing plastic clothes! Many materials used in clothes such as polyester, acrylic, viscose and nylon are made from plastics. But nylon was discovered by accident, too. Here's what happened.

A STRETCHY STORY

Nothing like it had ever been seen on Earth before. It was as strong as steel and ideal for bullet-proof vests. Yet its fibres were no thicker than a spider's web. It was made from nothing more sensational than petrol, natural gas, water and air.

The story began in 1928 when a mild-mannered, bespectacled chemist called Wallace Hume Carothers joined the giant DuPont Chemicals company at Delaware, USA.

"Young man," said Company Vice-President Charles Stine. "I've got a special job for you. We're looking at ways to make silk from minerals."

Most of us would say, "Yikes, that's a tall order!" But Corothers looked thoughtful. "I'll need to look at polymers. I mean those stringy molecules that make silk so strong and flexible. I wonder if it's possible?"

HECK – IF CATERPILLARS CAN DO IT SO CAN WE!

BLOOMING CHEEK!

"I guess the best way," said Carothers, "is to invent some new molecules."

"Well – that's your job, son. Just give it whatever it takes."

Carothers' lab was a chaotic maze of oddly-shaped flasks. There were tripods, jars filled with strange fluids and glass bottles with unreadable labels. But this is where he felt at home and where he made his great discovery.

After five years of research Carothers came up with his own substance – nylon. It was useless! Nylon was a clear plastic blob at the bottom of a test-tube. But it wouldn't melt unless you heated to a high temperature. So how could it be made into fibres suitable for a fabric?

Carothers turned his attention to polyesters. One day Julian Hill, one of Carothers' assistants, was mucking about with some polyester in a test-tube. He was amazed to find that he could pull strands of it out on a rod – like gungey mozzarella cheese on a cooked pizza.

'Let's wait till the boss goes out,' he told the others. 'I wanna try a little test.'

They pulled the stringy polyester as far they could. It must have been a strange sight as they managed to stretch it several metres down a corridor.

But this process locked the polyester molecules into place to form strong fibres. Maybe they could do the same for nylon? Yes, they certainly could.

This dramatic breakthrough made it possible to create amazing new fabrics. Carothers' reaction when he got back wasn't recorded but he might well have said, "It's good to see you're working at full stretch. Ha ha!"

Nylon stockings were launched at the World Trade Fair in 1938. A female audience heard Charles Stine declare, "It's the first man-made organic textile fibre … yet it's more elastic than any common natural fibres."

And the best news of all: nylon was going to be a lot cheaper than silk so more people could afford it. The audience were delighted and erupted into wild applause. They shouted and cheered until the ceiling shook. But Carothers wasn't there to see it…

A FATAL FINALE

In 1936 he had fallen into despair following the death of his sister. The following year he took his own life with a dose of the deadly poison cyanide. He was only 41 years old.

MORE MAN-MADE MARVELS

Within a few years the world would be at war and nylon was to prove itself a vital war-winning material. It was used to make countless parachutes and the used parachutes were then recycled to make stockings.

Nowadays, nylon is used to make not only stockings but everything from ropes and carpets to toothbrush bristles. Yet nylon is just one of hundreds of man-made substances. From A-Z they range from acrylic paints and zinc oxide (particularly useful for treating nappy rash).

Funnily enough – all these chemicals have something in common. They're made from atoms – those pesky little things that make chemists curious. Yup – it's time to get down to basics.

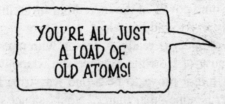

YOU'RE ALL JUST A LOAD OF OLD ATOMS!

AWESOME ATOMS

Atoms are awesome. Awesomely small that is. And awesomely important. After all, everything in the universe is made of them … including you.

THE INCREDIBLE SHRINKING TEACHER

The machine stands ready. It's an awesome jumble of tubes and lasers all polished and ready for use. All that's required is a brave and perhaps foolhardy volunteer to venture into the unknown. This person will experience the awesome power of the incredible shrinking ray – and hopefully live to tell the tale.

The volunteer is ready. A person with nerves of steel. In the cause of Horrible Science she is about to embark on what might prove to be a one way trip. This heroic volunteer is none other than … your science teacher.

She stands under the ray and seems to be disappearing. Soon she is no larger than a doll and she's still shrinking. In the blink of an eye she's become FIFTY times smaller. Now she's small enough to fit in your pocket! Then … is it an ant or a gnat? No, it's your teacher – and she's smaller than ever. Now she's FIVE HUNDRED times smaller. Hey – where's she gone now?

The smallest object you can see is about one tenth of a millimetre long. Your teacher is now tinier than this. If you had a microscope you might still see your teacher if she was 400 times smaller. But already she's too small for this. Now she's smaller even than the tiniest droplet sprayed from an aerosol can – 1/50,000th of a mm! And that's pretty small!

Your incredible shrinking teacher is falling, plunging headlong towards a mass of balls churning like a stormy sea. Every ball looks like a tiny planet surrounded by clouds of chaos. She's arrived in the weird world of atoms.

IT'S A SMALL WORLD

• You can stretch one million atoms in a line and they'd just about cover the full stop at the end of this sentence.

• If you squeezed them a bit you'd fit one billion billion – that's 1,000,000,000,000,000,000 atoms – onto a pin-head.

• You can fit 600,000,000,000,000,000,000,000 (that's six hundred billion trillion) atoms into a thimble.

But if atoms are so small, how do we know they exist?

Hall of fame: Democritus (c. 460–370 BC) Nationality: Greek

This ancient Greek was known as "the laughing philosopher" – no one knows why. He was certainly laughed at by some people for suggesting the existence of atoms. Here's his idea…

CUT A PIECE OF CHEESE IN HALF … CUT THE CHEESE IN HALF AGAIN AND AGAIN. EVENTUALLY YOU'LL GET A PIECE TOO SMALL TO CUT IN HALF. THAT'S AN ATOM!

In those days, few people imagined that atoms really existed so people poked fun at Democritus. But hundreds of years later he was proved right – so maybe he got the last laugh.

Bet you never knew!
Nowadays scientists can see atoms and even photograph them using a scanning tunnelling microscope. This brilliant bit of gizmo measures the electrical force between atoms at a single point. It produces amazing images that look strangely like table tennis balls!

INSIDE AN AWESOME ATOM

Here's an interesting thought: imagine your incredible shrinking teacher ventures inside an atom. Here's what she sees.

1 An atom is a blob of matter called a nucleus surrounded by electrons. The electrons are tiny bits of electrical energy.

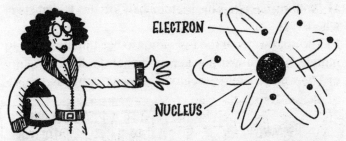

ELECTRON

NUCLEUS

2 Electrons zoom chaotically so that by the time you've spotted where they are they've moved somewhere else.

3 Mind you, the electrons can't go just anywhere. They're found in layers known as atomic orbitals.

Dare you discover ... how to watch atoms in action?

You will need:

Some water cooled in the fridge for two hours
Food colouring
A large glass

What you do:

1 Fill the glass half full with hot water.
2 Add a few drops of food colour and mix it up.

3 Fill the rest of the glass with the cold water. What happens?

a) Nothing at all. The bottom half of the water stays where it is.

b) The cold water at the top seems to be slipping down to mingle with the warm water in the bottom half.

c) The warm water seems to be moving upwards.

Answer: c) The warm water molecules are moving faster than the colder molecules. As they move apart they rise upwards. So you're seeing billions of atoms on the move.

The first problem for a chemist studying atoms is to work out how the atoms in a substance fit together. Now, the usual answer to this is to do lots of careful scientific experiments and then repeat them just to make sure they got it right. But one man had a different approach...

Hall of fame: Friedrich August Kekulé (1829–1896)
Nationality: German

At school Kekulé was good at drawing and he studied to be an architect. one day he went to a chemistry lecture by Justus von Liebig and got really excited about the subject although they never got on very well. So there you have it – you can still make a great discovery even if your teacher isn't your favourite person. According to the story Kekulé told many years later it all began when he was working as a research assistant in London.

A Dream Discovery

1. 1854. Kekulé was dozing on a double-decker bus.

2. All of a sudden he saw atoms dancing about.

3. Then he woke up.

4. But the dream had given him a nifty idea.

5. He decided to make model atoms using little balls joined by sticks.

THIS IS FUN!

That's how he figured out that carbon atoms can join together in straight chains to make new substances. It opened up a whole new field of chemistry. And all because of a dream!

6. 1863 Ghent, Belgium. Kekulé had another dream. He'd been writing a book whilst suffering a nasty dose of flu.

7. But he was also worrying about a tricky chemistry problem.

8. He dozed off and dreamt about snakes. Well, why not?

Benzene = a chemical in coal = 12 atoms. How are they arranged?

9. One of the snakes bit its own tail.

OUCH!

10. Kekulé awoke with a bright idea.

BENZENE IS RING-SHAPED

11. But many people thought this was a daft idea . . .

DREAM ON, KEKULÉ!

Today some experts think that Kekulé fibbed about his dreams to grab the glory for the benzene discovery from scientists who made the breakthrough before him. But it's definitely true that Kekulé spent years proving that benzene was indeed a ring of atoms. This dream discovery made it possible to develop new chemical dyes and thousands of other useful substances. Could you complete your chaotic chemistry homework in your sleep?

A DREAM COME TRUE!

ELEMENTARY CHAOS

Atoms come in over one hundred varieties. These different varieties are known as elements. For years chemical knowledge was in chaos as confused chemists tried to classify these chemicals. The idea of elements was invented by a boring British scientist – John Dalton.

Hall of fame: **John Dalton** (1766–1844) Nationality: British

John Dalton wasn't exactly a laugh-a-minute kind of bloke. He would drone on non-stop for hours about science, science and more science. And if that reminds you of a science teacher you know, you won't be too amazed to learn that John was a science teacher, too. They really did start young in those days. John was only 12 when he started teaching.

Like most other scientists, John knew that water could be broken down into hydrogen and oxygen. But those chemicals couldn't be broken down further. So he called them "elements" and said that each was a type of atom. People poked fun at John. But they were soon laughing on the other side of the faces. Scientists found that their experiments proved John right. He became famous and now there's even a statue of him.

ALWAYS KNEW I WAS RIGHT!

CHAOTIC CHEMICAL ELEMENTS

You can find 92 elements on Earth. More elements are made in nuclear reactors or created by scientists out of tiny bits of matter. But the heavier man-made elements have the rather irritating habit of falling apart after a second. Here's your very own chaotic guide to elements that don't do this.

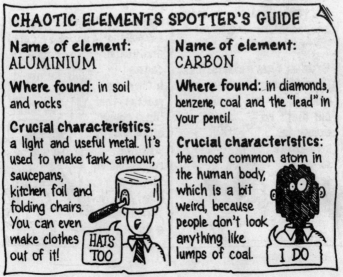

CHAOTIC ELEMENTS SPOTTER'S GUIDE

Name of element:
ALUMINIUM

Where found: in soil and rocks

Crucial characteristics: a light and useful metal. It's used to make tank armour, saucepans, kitchen foil and folding chairs. You can even make clothes out of it!

HATS TOO

Name of element:
CARBON

Where found: in diamonds, benzene, coal and the "lead" in your pencil.

Crucial characteristics: the most common atom in the human body, which is a bit weird, because people don't look anything like lumps of coal.

I DO

Name of element:
LEAD

Where found: This isn't the lead in your pencil. Real lead is a grey metal often found on old church roofs.

Crucial characteristics: it's quite a nasty poison if you happened to eat it by mistake. It's also very heavy so don't go dropping it on your teacher's toe.

Name of element:
CALCIUM

Where found: milk, chalk and marble and also in bones and the plaster used to set broken bones.

Crucial characteristics: if you burn calcium it gives off a lovely red flame. But that's no excuse for setting fire to your teacher's plastered toe!

OOH LOVELY!

Name of element:
CHLORINE

Where found: in salt, sea water and rock salt.

Crucial characteristics: it's very good for killing germs, but not very nice if it gets up your nose.

Name of element:
COPPER

Where found: in rocks under the ground.

Crucial characteristics: lots of uses including electrical wires and the rivets that hold your jeans together. Air pollution caused by cars and industry causes a chemical reaction that turns copper green. That's why the copper plated Statue of Liberty in New York looks a bit sea-sick.

GET ME A BUCKET

Name of element:
GOLD

Where found: in rocks under the ground.

Crucial characteristics: gold is good to make into jewellery – that's why people drape it round their necks. It's also worth lots of dosh.

Name of element:
HELIUM

Where found: in the air

Crucial characteristics: used to fill balloons. It's lighter than air so the balloons float skywards. Breathing helium makes your voice sound like Mickey Mouse. This happens because your voice passes faster through helium than ordinary air. So it sounds higher and squeakier!

Name of element:
HYDROGEN

Where found: it's the most common element. Stars such as the sun are made of hydrogen. So is 97 per cent of the known universe.

Crucial characteristics: hydrogen is also the lightest element so it floats upwards. This was why hydrogen gas was once used in balloons. It's also burnt as a rocket fuel. Hydrogen sulphide is a gas that stinks of rotten eggs. But don't confuse it with a stink bomb – it's poisonous.

Name of element:
IRON

Where found: much of the earth is made of iron. You find it in rocks and the soil.

Crucial characteristics: you can use iron to make railings. It's also found in the chemical that gives blood its tasteful red colour.

Name of element: OXYGEN

Where found: it's the most common element on Planet Earth.

Crucial characteristics: it's really lucky that over one fifth of the atoms in the air are oxygen. Without them we'd be more than a little bit dead. Some people think that if they breathe pure oxygen they'll live longer. They must be confused because scientists believe that breathing too much oxygen is bad for you. They say it damages the body, especially the nerves and lungs.

Name of element: PLUTONIUM

Where found: it's found in nuclear reactors but nowhere else in nature.

Crucial characteristics: Plutonium is incredibly poisonous. It looks like metal but it turns green in the air. And damp air makes it catch fire! The man who discovered plutonium in 1940 kept a lump of it in a matchbox. Weird.

Name of element: SILVER

Where found: in underground rocks.

Crucial characteristics: a really useful shiny metal much prized for dangling around the neck, making the shiny backs of mirrors and really posh cutlery. In the last 50 years people have lost 100,000 tonnes of silver coins. Where have they all got to? That's what I'd like to know.

I'VE NO IDEA – HONEST!

Name of element: SULPHUR

Where found: sulphur is a smelly yellow chemical spat out of volcanoes in choking clouds.

Crucial characteristics: at one time it was known as brimstone and mixed with treacle. It was used as a medicine for children. The medicine tasted disgusting so it was probably spat out by the choking children too.

ODD ELEMENTS QUIZ

Some of the more obscure elements are ever so odd. Which of these are too strange to be true?

True or false
1 The element phosphorous was discovered by an alchemist whilst he was examining the contents of his own urine.
2 The elements yttrium, erbium, terbium and ytterbium are all named after a quarry in Sweden.
3 The element dysprosium was discovered in 1886. The Greek name means "really smelly".

4 The element selenium was discovered by the Swedish scientist Berzelius. Sadly, he didn't realize it was poisonous until it poisoned him!

5 The element cadmium was discovered when it accidentally got into a bottle of medicine.
6 The element krypton was named after the planet that Superman comes from.

7 The scientist who discovered beryllium named it after his wife – Beryl.

8 The element Astatine is so rare that if you searched the entire world you'd only find 0.16 grams of it.

9 Technetium was first found in caterpillar droppings.

10 Lutetium is named after the ancient Roman name for Paris.

Answers: 1 Disgusting but TRUE. The alchemist was Hennig Brand (1630?–1692?, but nobody's really sure) and he made his discovery in 1669. It must have given him quite a shock – phosphorous glows in the dark. **2** TRUE. The place is called Ytterby and several elements were discovered there. **3** FALSE. It actually means "hard to get at". **4** TRUE. And unfortunately Berzelius died. **5** TRUE. In 1817 German chemist Friedrich Strohmeyer was analysing the chemicals in a bottle of medicine. **6** FALSE. But Krypton has been found floating around in space! The name means "secret" in Greek. **7** FALSE. **8** TRUE. It's the rarest of all the elements. **9** FALSE. **10** TRUE.

68

Hall of fame: Dmitri Mendeleyev (1834–1907)

Nationality: Russian

Other scientists had difficulties. But Mendeleyev lived a real-life soap opera. His father was a teacher who went blind. His mother ran the family glass factory and brought up 14 children. But when Dmitri was 14 the factory burnt down.

Dmitri went to St Petersburg to study chemistry. He discovered the Periodic Table by writing the elements on cards and arranging them as in his favourite card game – Patience. In 1955 element 101 was named mendelevium in his honour. So Dmitri ended up in his own Table!

THE COMPLICATED BIT

So that's it. All you need to know is the Periodic Table and which elements join together. Simple, really? Er – no. Just to add a little chaos – chemicals are always changing and getting mixed up. Confused? You soon will be. See you in the next chapter!

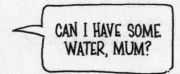

CHAOTIC CHEMICAL CHANGES

Everything changes – this fact is so well known it's a cliché. But WHY exactly do things change? Well, with chemicals it's mainly due to the effects of heat or cold. This can result in a few chaotic chemical mix-ups.

Bet you never knew!
You might think that water is runny, iron is solid, and oxygen is a gas. Wrong, wrong and WRONG again! In fact ANY chemical can be a solid, a liquid or a gas. It just depends on how hot the chemical is at the time. Below 0°C (32°F) water is the solid object we call ice. Above that temperature water turns into ... well ... water and above 100°C (212°F) water boils and turns into a mixture of gas and tiny droplets – you'd probably call it steam.

SOLID SECRETS

Have you ever wondered why some solid objects are bendy and others are very tough? Well, have you ever pondered why your auntie's best china is always breaking and why her rock cakes are ... just like rocks? Here's the answer.

- In every solid object the atoms are bonded together. But what's important is the way the atoms are arranged.
- If they're in stretchy strings the object will be stretchy like an elastic band. You can squash them together quite easily.

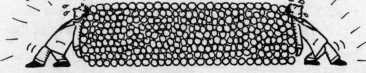

- In very hard materials such as diamonds the atoms are arranged in a very tight and very strong framework.

- In softer materials such as graphite – pencil lead – the atoms are arranged in loose layers that rub off easily when you write.

- In china the atoms are closely packed and joined tightly together. But if just one atomic join breaks the china will crack!

- In a metal the atoms are surrounded by a crowd of jostling electrons. (They're a bit like teachers in a playground at break-time.) The electrical force of the electrons keeps the atoms in place. But each atom can move a bit and that's why you can bend metal – if you're very strong!

MELTING MOMENTS

Here are some impressive facts about melting and freezing water.

1 In Northern Canada some lakes freeze solid. The freezing starts with a single ice-crystal that grows and grows. So each frozen lake becomes a giant ice-crystal.

2 As water freezes it expands and crushes anything it traps with a force of 140 kg per square cm. That's enough to sink a ship or crush a man to death!

3 You get snow and hail when water molecules join and freeze in the sky. Hailstones occur when lumps of ice swirl around in a cold cloud getting larger and larger. In June 2003 a hailstone as large as a soccer ball fell on Nebraska, USA.

4 You can make snowballs because snow is partly melted ice and slushy so you can squash the snow together. If it's really cold, as in the Antarctic, the snow is hard and powdery.

So you can't have a snowball fight at the South Pole.

5 Here's what happens when you melt ice... When they are stuck together as ice the water molecules are fairly still although they do wobble a bit.

6 It's only when a chemical is really cold that the molecules stop moving completely. This temperature is -273.15°C (-459.67°F), absolute zero.

7 As ice melts the molecules take in heat energy and wobble about more and more. Then they wobble free and start floating around.

WOBBLING MOLECULE

MELTING ICE CUBE

YIPPEE!

FREE AT LAST!

8 As they heat up even more, they move faster and faster until they take a flying leap into the air and become a gas.

Bet you never knew!

1 Different chemicals melt and turn into gases at different temperatures. It's all to do with the bonds between atoms in the chemical. If these bonds are strong you need loads of heat energy to break them apart. So their melting point is higher.

2 All gases need to be very cold before they become liquids. To make liquid oxygen you need to cool it to -188.191°C (-306.74°F). And to make solid oxygen it needs to be a very chilly -218.792°C (-361.83°F)! Luckily, our weather isn't that cold or we'd have nothing to breathe. And that would cause chaos!

TEST YOUR TEACHER

Of course, anything can be a liquid – if it's the right temperature. Terrorize your teacher with this terribly tricky test.

1 Over hundreds of years glass sinks slowly to the bottom of a window frame. Does that make glass a liquid or solid?

2 The black displays that you get in some calculators are made out of crystals – are they a liquid or solid?

3 Is school custard a liquid or a solid?

NOT SURE – I'LL CHEW IT OVER

4 If you cool helium gas to -271°C (-455°F) it can be poured and it even climbs up the sides of a beaker. Is it liquid or solid?

Answers: 1 It's a liquid! **2** Trick question. They're special molecules that exist somewhere in-between. **3** It's a liquid called a colloid – that's a liquid with lots of little oily drops in. Yuck! You can squash custard powder mixed with water into a solid – if you're brave enough, that is! **4** Another trick question. It's a supercool liquid which explains why it acts rather oddly.

MIXED-UP MIXTURES

Much of our planet is made up of mixed-up chemicals. Take a breath of air. In one gulp you'll get a chaotic combination of oxygen, nitrogen and hydrogen and a few other gases thrown in for good measure. All these atoms are completely mixed up, but guess what? The funny thing is that nothing happens, there's no reaction between them, so you don't notice them all.

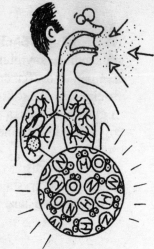

When you mix two gases or two liquids, the atoms of each chemical often spread out until they are thoroughly mixed. But some mixtures don't mix properly.

If a liquid is heavier than water it may sink to the bottom of a glass of water and not mix with it at all. Try out this chaotic chemical cocktail...

You will need:
A tall glass
Water (adding a few drops of food colouring might make it more interesting)
Oil
Syrup (in roughly equal amounts)
Umbrella (optional)
Straw (optional)

What you do:
1 Pour a similar amount of each of the three liquids into the glass.
2 Sit around and wait for something to happen.
3 Check your answer against these three possibles...

a) The liquids all mix together.

b) The water stays at the top, the oil sinks to the middle and the syrup to the bottom.

c) The oil rises to the top, the water stays in the middle and the syrup sinks to the bottom.

Answer: c) Unless you've gone chaotically wrong somewhere.

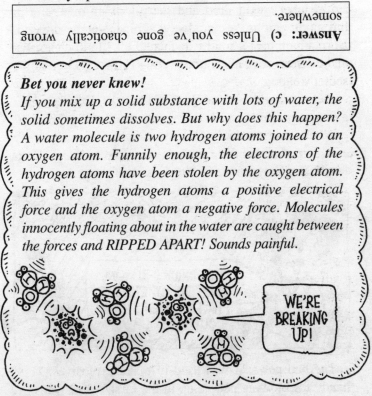

Bet you never knew!

If you mix up a solid substance with lots of water, the solid sometimes dissolves. But why does this happen? A water molecule is two hydrogen atoms joined to an oxygen atom. Funnily enough, the electrons of the hydrogen atoms have been stolen by the oxygen atom. This gives the hydrogen atoms a positive electrical force and the oxygen atom a negative force. Molecules innocently floating about in the water are caught between the forces and RIPPED APART! Sounds painful.

WE'RE BREAKING UP!

UN-MIXING MIXTURES

Not only can you mix up chemicals, much of the time you can un-mix them too. For example, if a substance is mixed with water you can boil off the water and you're left with the original chemical. Talking about un-mixing things from water – one scientist had a very funny idea about this. He was Germany's Fritz Haber and here's his story…

Hall of fame: Fritz Haber (1868–1934) Nationality: German

Fritz Haber was a short and sharp-looking man, and in old photographs he is always immaculately dressed. Born a merchant's son he dedicated his life to chemistry and the service of his country. Yes – Fritz was Germany's secret weapon.

Before the First World War (1914–1918) Fritz invented a new way to make a chemical called ammonia. This had good and bad results.

• The good news: the ammonia was used to make cheap fertilizers. Very handy for helping plants to grow.

• The bad news: it was used to make explosives. Very handy for blowing people up in the First World War.

Eventually the Germans lost the war. The country was in a mess and nearly penniless. And that's when Fritz had his funny idea.

FRITZ GOES GOLD HUNTING

If you really want to raise a few billion dollars don't wash your dad's car on a Sunday afternoon. Go prospecting for gold instead! There's gold in that there sea – millions of tons of clinky-clanky yellow stuff! Think about it … 71 per cent of the Earth is covered by oceans with 97 per cent of all the world's water. Imagine millions of streams scouring gold from rocks and crevices and rivers washing it down to the sea!

But there's one teeny little problem. The gold is in tiny little atoms and grains. They're mixed up with trillions of tonnes of water, salts and all the 70 or so other chemicals you get dissolved in the sea.

In the previous 50 years no fewer than 50 scientists had come up with inventions for removing the gold. And they ALL failed!

But Fritz and his fellow scientists were all keen to have a go. So they chartered a luxury ocean liner called the *Hansa* and set sail in search of gold-rich seawater. The plan was to boil off the water and use other chemicals to separate the gold from the solid dregs.

But after three voyages and eight years they gave up. Here's the cause of their chaos. If you searched a billion buckets of seawater you'd find traces of gold in only 40 – if you were LUCKY! There's loads of gold in the sea but there's even more seawater. And getting the gold ain't worth the effort.

But that's not the last we'll hear of Fritz. He pops up rather nastily in the next chapter.

IT'S A GAS!

Without gases there'd be chaos. We'd have nothing to breathe and balloons would fall out of the sky. Gases can be chaotic – especially when they poison people or explode! But they're interesting, too. Sometimes they're even funny – take nitrous oxide, for example, better known to you as laughing gas.

. . . MY CAT WAS RUN OVER

. . . THE CAR WAS STOLEN

. . . AND OUR HOUSE BURNT DOWN!

Chemical chaos fact file

Name: Gases

The basic facts: Gases are atoms or clumps of atoms that whiz about like tiny balls. You can feel the gas atoms in the air every time you go out in a wind.

Horrible details: Some gases are poisonous. (See next few pages for details.)

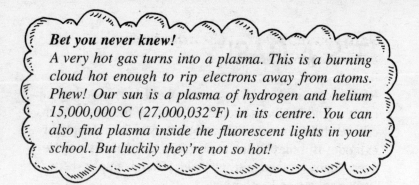
STINK BOMBS

Some chemists don't smell too good. This must be true otherwise they wouldn't produce such stinky substances. Any smell is caused by gas molecules which we sniff in the air. Now *you* can kick up a bit of a stink using...

There are thousands of stinks known to chemists but the worst are ethyl-mercaptan (e-thile-mare-cap-tan) and butyl seleno-mercaptan (bu-tile see-le-no-mare-cap-tan). The first reeks of leeks and is poisonous. The second stinks like rotten cabbage, rotten cabbage, garlic, onions, burnt toast and sewer gas ALL MIXED TOGETHER! Phwoar!

But if you fancy something even more nasty, try "Who me?" US chemists came up with this putrid pong during the Second World War. The plan was for French Resistance agents to spray the stinky stuff on German solders to embarrass them! Trouble was the stinky spray made the agents just as smelly.

Dare you discover … gas experiments?

1 Want to grab a bit of gas?

You will need:

A balloon

What you do:

1 Blow up the balloon and pinch the end with your fingers.

2 Squeeze the balloon.

What happens?

a) As you squash more the balloon gets harder to squeeze.

b) As you squash more the balloon gets softer.

c) The balloon stays the same.

2 Make your own gas

You will need:

A narrow-necked bottle half-filled with water

A balloon (use the same one!)

2 alka-seltzer tablets crushed into powder

Funnel

What you do:

1 Blow the balloon up and release the air a few times to make it softer.

2 Use the funnel to pour the powdered tablets into the bottle.

3 Quickly stretch the balloon over the neck of the bottle.

4 Very gently swirl the water around in the bottle.

What happens?

a) The balloon is sucked into the bottle.

b) There is a small explosion.

c) The balloon inflates slightly.

3 Bubble trouble

You will need:

A bottle of fizzy mineral water, lemonade or cola.

What you do:

Give the bottle a really good shake for two minutes. *Slowly* open the top and notice what happens.

a) Nothing

b) Loads of bubbles form and gas escapes.

c) Bubbles appear then sink to the bottom.

Answers: 1 a) Billions of gas atoms are squashed together. The harder you squeeze, the harder those atoms push back! **2 c)** The tablets react with water to make carbon-dioxide gas. The molecules of this gas are made from one carbon and two oxygen atoms joined together. **3 b)** The fizz comes from carbon-dioxide bubbles. The gas is dissolved in water under pressure. Removing the top reduces pressure and allows bubbles to form.

Bet you never knew!

Just as in experiment 3 gas bubbles form in the blood of deep sea divers as they surface. The "bends" as they are called can have fatal results! To prevent this, divers spend time in a pressurized chamber so their bodies get used to the change in pressure.

WHAT A GAS!

The air is mainly made of nitrogen. Some plants use this to help them grow though it doesn't do much for us. But the oxygen and carbon dioxide in the air are worth gassing about.

Hall of fame: Joseph Priestley (1733–1804)

Nationality: British

Priestley's friend Sir Humphry Davy said:

No single person has ever discovered so many new and curious substances

GOSH!

(Not since the first scientific analysis of school dinners anyway.) Joe could speak nine languages but he was useless at maths. In the 1790s Priestley disagreed with the Government and his political enemies sent a mob to smash up his lab. The shaken scientist did a runner to the USA. Could you think like Priestley? Try explaining the results of one of his famous experiments.

A LOAD OF HOT AIR

1 In 1674 scientist John Mayow put a mouse in a jar with a candle.

2 The mouse fainted as the candle burnt out.

3 In 1771 Priestley burnt a candle in a jar until the flame went out. Then he added a sprig of mint to the jar.

4 The plant stayed healthy.

5 A few months later Priestley added a mouse. This time the mouse stayed awake.

6 Finally the scientist added a candle in the jar again. The candle burnt normally, the plant stayed healthy and the mouse stayed awake.

So how do you explain these results?

a) The mouse produced a gas that the plant used. The candle also used this gas.

b) The plant used a gas made by the candle and produced another gas that the mouse used.

c) The candle made a gas that the mouse and the plant both used.

In 1774 Priestley heated mercuric oxide to make a colourless non-smelly gas. He put this gas in a jar and added a mouse. The mouse seemed happy and relaxed. So Priestley sniffed the gas.

AHA! THE RODENT SEEMETH CONTENTED

SNIFF SNIFF

Which gas was it?

a) The gas produced by the plant.

b) The gas produced by the candle.

c) The gas produced by the mouse.

Answer: a) In 1783 Priestley's friend Lavoisier (later to lose his head) found that the gas from the candle was the same gas breathed out by the mouse. Its name is carbon dioxide. Lavoisier called Priestley's other gas – the one made from mercuric oxide – "oxygen".

Bet you never knew!
Joseph Priestley invented fizzy drinks. He put together a home-made machine from a washing tub and a few wine glasses and bubbled carbon dioxide through water. The water tasted fizzy and you could flavour it with fruit juices. But Priestley stored the gas in a pig's bladder and funnily enough some people complained that the drink had a "piggy" flavour.

TRICK QUESTION FOR YOUR TEACHER.
Who discovered oxygen – Priestley or Lavoisier?

Answer: Neither. Oxygen had been discovered some years before by Swedish scientist Karl Scheele.

Hall of fame: Karl Scheele (1746–1786) Nationality: Swedish
Karl Scheele discovered new chemicals such as oxygen, chlorine and nitrogen. But life wasn't much of a gas for

this sad scientist. Owing to a publishing mix-up the book describing his discoveries wasn't printed for 28 years! Meanwhile, other chemists had discovered the same chemicals. And to make matters even worse, Scheele died after being poisoned by a chemical he discovered but never got the credit for!

A MAD MACHINE

Meanwhile scientists investigated hydrogen gas. The lighter-than-air hydrogen was ideal for filling balloons but early flying machines were fearsomely fatal. In 1785 French balloon pioneer Pilâtre de Rozier was killed trying to fly this chaotic contraption. A faulty valve probably caused the crash.

In 1819 balloonist Sophie Blanchard was killed when her hydrogen balloon caught fire. Some of the watching crowd cheered. They thought the blaze was part of the act.

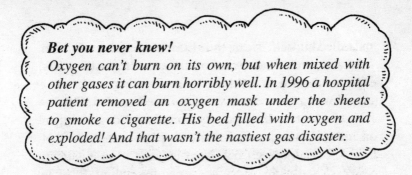

THE LAST LAUGH

Sir Humphry Davy (1778–1829) was 19 when he discovered laughing gas, or nitrous oxide as the chemists call it. He thought there was something funny about the gas when he sniffed it. And he felt so good that he burst into gales of laughter.

Laughing gas shows became a popular form of entertainment. You could see people sniffing the gas and making fools of themselves. In 1839 a chemist described how people breathed the gas out of pigs' bladders:

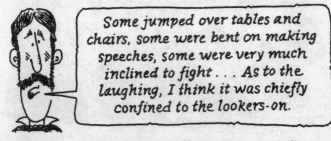

Some jumped over tables and chairs, some were bent on making speeches, some were very much inclined to fight . . . As to the laughing, I think it was chiefly confined to the lookers-on.

And the funny thing was that people under the influence of the gas didn't seem to feel any pain.

THE DABBLING DENTIST

Ambitious American dentist Horace Wells (1815–1848) experimented unsuccessfully with laughing gas as a way of knocking people out for operations. Later he went mad and killed himself. Meanwhile his former partner William T Morton the proud owner of a false teeth factory, was experimenting with another chemical – ether.

Following the advice of a professor called Charles Jackson, Morton tested the gas on his pet dog and then on himself. Mind you, I don't suppose he noticed that he'd knocked himself out. Next he tried it on a patient. Success! Sadly, this story has a painful ending. Ether is quite cheap and easy to make. So to make money Morton said he'd invented a brand new substance.

He coloured the ether pink and added perfumes to it so no one would recognize it. Then he sold the bottles to doctors at ludicrous prices. He thought he'd be laughing all the way to the bank. But when the doctors found out they'd been cheated, they lost all confidence in Morton.

Morton exchanged a lot of hot air in his arguments with Charles Jackson over who had discovered ether. One day the inventor read a magazine article crediting Jackson with the discovery. He was so cross he had a fit and died. Meanwhile, Jackson had been acting rather oddly. After a visit to Morton's grave he went mad and had to be locked up.

In the last fifty years laughing gas has come back into fashion. It has been widely used as a painkiller in hospitals.

So I suppose Horace Wells got the last laugh.

And if you think this story sounds chaotic, wait till you get wind of these nasty niffs…

THE MOST HORRIBLE GAS COMPETITION

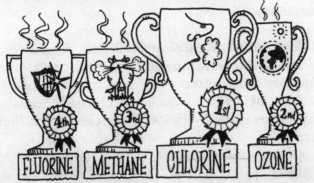

FOURTH PRIZE

Fluorine Five scientists tried to make this gas – all were poisoned. Eventually French scientist Henri Moissan (1852–1907) succeeded using platinum equipment. Platinum is one of the few materials fluorine doesn't dissolve.

Nowadays, tiny safe amounts of fluorine atoms are found in the chemicals called fluorides in toothpaste that help protect teeth from decay. That's OK, but too much fluoride actually discolours teeth.

THIRD PRIZE

Methane gas bubbling from marshes catches fire to make the ghostly lights called will-o'-the-wisps or jack-o'-lanterns. You'll also find methane in cows' farts (and humans') – *and* the gas that people use for cooking. It's true!

SECOND PRIZE · RUNNER UP

Ozone gas molecules are formed by three oxygen atoms joined together. They smell of new-mown hay and were discovered when a scientist noticed a funny pong in his lab.

Ozone kills germs. It also kills people if they breathe too much of it. Luckily most ozone is 25 km up in the air where it forms a useful barrier against the sun's harmful rays.

WINNER (JUST NOSING AHEAD)

Chlorine In the 1980s scientists spotted a hole in the ozone layer over Antarctica. The gap was caused by pollution by CFCs – chemicals containing chlorine. The hole grew until by the 2000s it was bigger than North America.

But this horrible yellow-green gas has been causing problems for centuries. Over 600 years ago an alchemist bubbled chlorine though water and said it was good for salad dressings. WRONG. Chlorine is horribly poisonous.

In the First World War German scientist Fritz Haber developed chlorine gas as a horrible weapon of war...

A BREATH OF AIR

"Tell me about it," Billy pleaded.

Arthur McAllsop hunched his shoulders against the cold drizzle and shook his head. "I've told you son – it's not a nice story."

"You said you'd look after me."

"Yeah, I did. Listen son, just keep your head down and you'll be alright."

"Well, I need to know about it. Can't have been too bad – you're still here aren't you?"

A flare cut through the night. Billy blinked in the sudden blaze of light. He looked so young – just 16 and his first time away from home. Must have lied about his age.

Arthur sighed. There was nothing for it. The boy would find out soon enough.

"We were near Ypres, I expect you've heard of the fights there in 1915. Well, it was a quiet sort of day – warm for April. Nothing much to bother us all day. We were having a nice cup of tea when it happened."

"What happened?" asked Billy.

"Gas," said Arthur. "The gas attack. It was like a yellow fog rolling down. Well, luckily the wind blew the worst of it away. We didn't have gas masks then."

"Did you get gassed?"

"Only a bit. It was like a horrible sore throat and I couldn't stop coughing. But I was lucky – I was still alive."

"That night it poured with rain. The shelling didn't let up. Not for one moment. Chaos. You couldn't hear yourself talk. We had nothing to eat, no sleep. After we came out of the line everything was a mess. The gas had turned all the grass yellow. And there were no birds in the trees."

There was a long silence. It was a quiet night and if you listened hard you could hear voices from the enemy trenches. Orders in a foreign language. Then came a crack of rifle fire and the whine of a stray bullet.

"Arthur, you don't think they'd use gas on us?"

Both men sniffed the air. The trench smelled of mouldy earth. Muddy water squelched on the duckboards beneath their army boots.

"No Billy – we'll be all right. They put the gas in shells now. They don't blow up but they do go plop! So if one plops you'd better put your gas mask on double-quick!"

It was getting lighter and a chill dawn breeze set the barbed wire twanging. Soon it would be time to stand to – then they could eat breakfast.

The soldiers heard the approaching shell. It whistled through the air like a train getting louder and louder. They both crouched, instinctively ducking their heads.

Waiting for the bang that never came. Instead the shell fell in the mud of No Man's Land with a gentle plop.

Billy turned white.

"Gas," he cried in a choking voice. "GAS!"

In seconds the word was passed down the line. Half-awakened soldiers groaned and cursed – fumbling with the clumsy gas masks they wore around their necks.

Only one man did nothing. A man who had already seen the worst of gas warfare and knew what to expect.

"Don't be silly, Billy!" cried Arthur McAllsop. "It's a dud shell. Gas shells don't whistle like that!"

Bet you never knew!
1 By the end of the First World War more then 125,000 tonnes of gas had been released by both the British and the Germans.
2 The first gas masks were rifle cleaning cloths soaked in urine (the water in the urine was supposed to absorb the gas). Yuck!
3 Eventually the soldiers were given gas masks that absorbed the gas in layers of charcoal.
4 In 1975 Dr Buddy Lapidus used this idea to invent odour-eating insoles. The charcoal eats up nasty smelly foot odour like a little gas mask!

But gases aren't the only deadly chemicals. Metals make murderous weapons, too.

MARVELLOUS MURDEROUS METALS

What's hard, shiny and doesn't bounce when it hits the floor? No, it's not your teacher's bald head, although it could be – it's a metal! Where would we be without metals? Think of the chaos it would cause. We'd have no coins, cars or computers for a start. But then we'd also have less in the way of murderous weapons. Let's face the facts...

Chemical chaos fact file

Name: Metals

The basic facts: In a metal the atoms aren't actually joined together – they're surrounded by a crowd of electrons. This allows you to bend metals and stretch them into wires.

Horrible details: Some metals have horrible habits. Two called rubidium and caesium must be kept away from water to stop them exploding!

HOW MUCH FOR THE UMBRELLA?

RUBIDIUM

CAESIUM

But metals have many amazing secrets too!

MARVELLOUS METAL FACTS

1 Some metals can float on water – for example, sodium does until it reacts with the water to make hydrogen gas.

2 Mercury is a metal that is actually a liquid at room temperature. You can see it in your thermometer. As the mercury heats up, it expands up the scale. Mind you – one Russian winter the thermometers all froze at -38°C. If your school ever gets that cold it's time to go home!

3 Gallium melts so easily that if you put some in your hand it collapses into a greasy puddle!

4 Tantalum is a rare grey metal used to make plates that cover holes in the skull.

5 Nowadays, platinum is more valuable than gold. But the funny thing is that in the sixteenth century the Spanish government thought the metal could be made into fake coins. So they dumped their entire stock of platinum in the sea!

6 In 1800 William H Wollaston (1766–1828) invented a way to re-shape platinum into long threads so it could be made into new shapes. The cunning chemist was raking in cash like crazy from his invention and made sure no one else found out. The secret was revealed after he died. Well – he didn't need the money any more!

7 Titanium is a metal that doesn't melt easily. This is good for making fast aircraft because their wings get very hot due to air molecules rubbing over them at high speed.

8 Scientists have suggested making artificial legs out of titanium. At least they won't buckle under in the heat of the sun!

SENSATIONAL SILVER

Silver is so widely used it's difficult to believe that anything could be so useful. Which of these silver adverts are too stupid to be true?

a PROBLEMS WITH PAINFUL JOINTS?
Take these real silver pills. Genuine cure promised.

b Are your knuckle joints wearing out? Replace them today with this lovely silver set. Invest for the future!

c Jet engine for sale – genuine solid silver bits in it.

d Problems with germs? A silver water tank kills germs and keeps your water fresher for longer.

e LOVELY SILVER SOLAR PANELS. Now you can live on the sunny side of the street.

f BURNS ARE A PAIN! Take this soothing silver lotion. Guaranteed healing!

Answers: All are TRUE except b)!

AMAZING ALUMINIUM

Apart from silver, aluminium is one of the most useful metals known to man. But aluminium was once amazingly difficult and expensive to make. The French Emperor Napoleon III had his cutlery and baby's rattle made out of aluminium just to show how wealthy he was!

Hall of fame: Charles M Hall (1863–1914) Nationality: American
Paul L T Héroult (1863–1914) Nationality: French
One day Charlie heard his teacher say,

THE PERSON WHO DISCOVERS HOW TO MAKE CHEAP ALUMINIUM WILL BECOME RICH AND FAMOUS

GEE WHIZ!

So the go-getting young American decided to have a go. Soon he was hard at work on his main piece of equipment . . . a grotty old gas stove in a woodshed.

Against all the odds – Charlie succeeded! The trick is to dissolve aluminium-rich bauxite in a chemical called cryolite. Amazingly this discovery was made at the same time by Frenchman Paul Héroult. Both inventors were exactly the same age and both worked in similarly chaotic chemistry labs! And here's the really bizarre bit. They were born and died in the same year too! Aluminium may be amazing, but it's not...

AS GOOD AS GOLD

Yes – GOLD. It's the stuff that dreams are made of. Royal crowns, pirate treasure, ancient coins. For thousands of years men have fought, struggled and died to get their mits on this magical metal. And sometimes they've made complete fools of themselves...

FOOL'S GOLD

Sir Martin Frobisher (1537?–1596) was nobody's fool. The tough-talking Yorkshireman was everyone's idea of an explorer – brave, weather-beaten and determined.

In 1576 Frobisher sailed off in search of a sea route to Asia across the north of Canada. Sir Martin didn't find the fabled route but he did visit the icy wilderness of Baffin Island. And there he made a stunning discovery.

It was a lump of rock that glittered in the chilly northern sun! Back in England two experts confirmed it, "Yup – it's gold." Chaos soon ensued because everyone wanted to grab a share.

The next year, Frobisher returned to the island with a larger expedition. It was no picnic – they braved icebergs and gales that could tear a ship to pieces. On land there were polar bears strong enough to kill a man with a single blow. But it was worth the danger. Working with picks in the freezing cold, they hacked away 197 tonnes of the golden rock.

The following year Frobisher headed an armada full of excited adventurers. This time the ships returned laden with an incredible 1,180 tonnes of the glittering prize. It was worth a fortune – enough to make them rich beyond their wildest dreams. Or so they reckoned…

Then the bubble burst. There was no gold on Baffin Island. It was just iron pyrite – a common-as-muck mixture of iron ore and sulphur that you can find anywhere. Some unkind people called it "fool's gold". Sir Martin and his crew became a laughing stock.

Would you have been fooled by iron pyrite? Here are a few tips to make sure you get the right stuff.

BECOME A GOLD PROSPECTOR

1 Panning for gold

Swirl a load of sand and water in a pan. Carefully swill the water and floating sand from the pan. Any gold will settle to the bottom of the pan as golden grains or nuggets.

2 Testing for gold

Scrape your golden nugget on a dark rock called a touchstone. If it leaves a streak of gold it's genuine.

3 Dig a gold mine

It takes time to dig your own mine. Some mines are thousands of metres deep so don't dig into your garden unless you're sure there's real gold lurking in the rocks beneath. You have got real gold in the rocks beneath your garden? OK, then, here's how to get at it.

Getting the gold . . .

1 You'll need to spend a lot of money on machines, etc. One million pounds should cover it.

2 Smash thousands of tonnes of rock with heavy machines. Check every bit of rock to make sure you don't chuck away the golden nuggets by mistake. (You wouldn't see the funny side of this.)

3 Then smash them up in a giant cylinder filled with ball-bearings. (It's much quicker than using a potato masher.)

4 Mix the rock powder with the deadly poison cyanide plus water to make a slimy mess. (Don't try this in the living room.)

5 Leave the slime to settle in a tank. Then remove any bits of rock. Check for gold.

6 Add zinc dust to the slime. This separates out the cyanide from any gold there.

7 Melt the gold with a chemical called borax. The borax sticks to any unwanted chemicals and floats to the top of the mixture. Carefully skim this off.

8 A bit of further processing and you end up with a bar of 99.6% gold. It's as simple as that! (NOT)

Now you've gone to all this trouble to get gold, what do you do with it? Oddly enough, you might put it back underground – in a bank vault. That's where half the world's gold ends up!

Bet you never knew!
In the 1920s gold was used in medicines to kill off the lung disease tuberculosis, but it poisoned the patients too. Yes, there's a mean side to metals. In fact, you could call them murderous.

MURDEROUS METAL POISONS

Lead is dangerous. Sixteenth-century ladies used white lead face powder to improve their complexions. After a few years the poison ruined their skin – it absorbed the lead and gave them blood poisoning. But the ladies didn't know why their skin was ruined so they used extra lead to cover up the damage!

YEAR 1   YEAR 2   YEAR 3   YEAR 4

But the most poisonous metal in the world is arsenic. Many years ago this substance was used to make fly papers. Flies stuck to the paper and came to a sticky end once the arsenic got to work. Unfortunately a few humans went the same way too.

Mind you, poison isn't the only way that metals can murder people. Metals make lethal weapons too.

Murderous metal weapons

1. The first iron weapons were made from meteorites that fell from outer space.

2. Ancient people worked out how to heat iron-ore to make metal, but it wasn't very strong.

3. Iron needed to be mixed with another metal before it was really strong. In 1400BC people first added carbon to iron to make it stronger.

ONE PORTION OF CARBON

4. Meanwhile soldiers fought with bronze swords. But they often bent in battle!

HA HA HA

5. Iron swords were much harder, sharper . . . and more deadly.

SWOOSH

And that wasn't all. There followed iron guns and iron cannon firing iron cannon balls. This led to more chaos on the battlefield and buckets of blood being spilt. And oddly enough, there's iron in blood too.

CHAOTIC CHEMICAL EXPRESSIONS

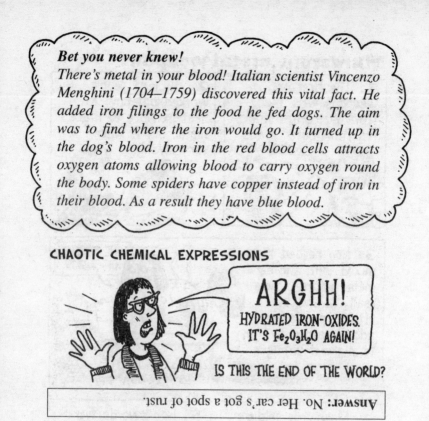

ARGHH!
HYDRATED IRON-OXIDES.
IT'S $Fe_2O_3H_2O$ AGAIN!

IS THIS THE END OF THE WORLD?

Answer: No. Her car's got a spot of rust.

A ROTTEN REACTION

One big problem with iron is that it joins up with oxygen atoms to make rust. That's right – rust is a compound of iron and oxygen atoms. And rusting is speeded up by water and salt. This is why rusty old ships sail the salty seas.

And rusting is just one of many rotten reactions.

RUST IS A MIXTURE OF IRON AND OXYGEN ATOMS – WATER AND SALT ACCELERATE THE PROCESS, BLAH BLAH...

SHUT UP AND KEEP BAILING MAN!

ROTTEN REACTIONS

What have rusting and rotting got in common with photography? Give up? They're all based on chemical reactions. But what exactly is a chemical reaction?

Chemical chaos fact file

Name: Chemical Reactions

The basic facts: A chemical reaction is when atoms join together – or joined-up atoms split apart so new chemicals appear.

Horrible details: Rusting isn't the only rotten reaction caused by oxygen. Oxygen mixed with butter or margarine over time makes them revoltingly rancid! It's enough to wipe the smile off anyone's face.

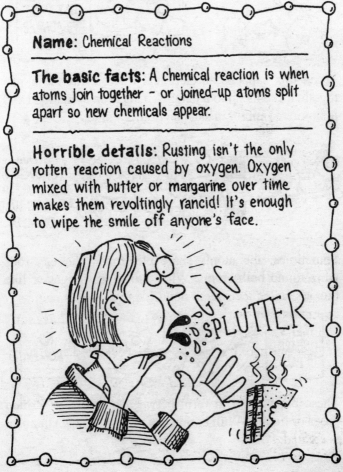

QUICK REACTIONS

Normally, when atoms bump into one another they bounce apart again. But if they're moving fast they can stick together before they have a chance to rebound. The outer groups of electrons decide what happens next... Sometimes atom kindly gives the other its electrons.

When this happens an electrical force sticks the atoms together like metal to a magnet. This is an ionic bond and it's more common in salts and other minerals.

Sometimes, the atoms share electrons. The electrons whiz round both atoms. When atoms join together like this it's called a covalent bond.

These bonds tend to form between non-metals – often gases or liquids. With both types of bond a new chemical is created.

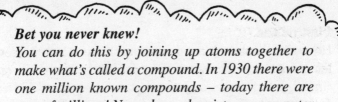

PREDICTABLE REACTIONS

So atoms bump together and decide to join up. It sounds hit or miss doesn't it? But it isn't. Do you remember Mendeleyev playing Patience in the chapter, "Elementary chaos"? Thanks to Mendeleyev's Periodic Table, scientists can predict what happens. It's so simple. It just depends on the number of electrons an atom has in its outer atomic orbital – that's the outer layer that electrons can move in. If you have an adverse reaction to this, you shouldn't try this puzzle.

ROTTEN REACTION PUZZLE

Here are the atoms you'll be using to work out the puzzles.

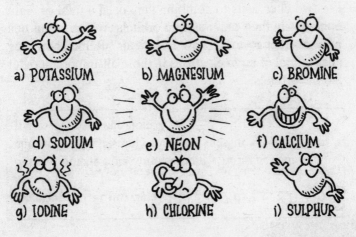

a) POTASSIUM b) MAGNESIUM c) BROMINE

d) SODIUM e) NEON f) CALCIUM

g) IODINE h) CHLORINE i) SULPHUR

First puzzle

How many outer electrons does each atom have? Read the clues below then work it out for all the atoms above. *Clues:*

1 Sulphur has six electrons – that's three times more electrons than calcium. But between them they've enough to make a new chemical.

2 Neon has the same number of electrons as sulphur and calcium combined.

3 Magnesium has twice as many electrons as sodium and potassium.

4 Sodium and chlorine have enough electrons to make a chemical called sodium chloride. That's salt to you.

5 But sodium has only half as many electrons as calcium.

6 All the other atoms have one less electron than neon.

Second puzzle

For two chemicals to combine they need a total of eight electrons in their outer atomic orbitals. Which atoms can join together to make new chemicals? Remember, they need a total of eight electrons in those all-important outer atomic orbitals.

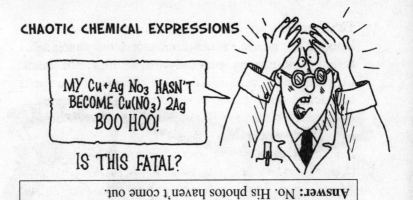

MY Cu + Ag NO₃ HASN'T BECOME Cu(NO₃) 2Ag BOO HOO!

IS THIS FATAL?

Answer: No. His photos haven't come out.

GET THE PICTURE!

You might think these chemical reactions are a bit remote from everyday life. Surely you'd never normally have a hand in a reaction? But if you took a photo with a traditional light-based camera – you would need a chemical reaction to get the picture!

1 The first photographers used light-sensitive silver chloride paper. Energy from light causes a reaction that turns the silver chloride black.

2 Light showed up as dark on the photograph. Dark patches showed up as white.

3 To be in a photo you had to sit still and wait for the chemical action to work. This could take hours and meanwhile you had to keep a totally straight face!

GOSH IS THAT THE TIME? NOW JUST STAY STILL FOR AN HOUR WHILE I HAVE MY LUNCH

4 Unfortunately the chemicals continued to react to light so you had to look at your photographs in the dark!

5 This problem was overcome when inventors discovered a chemical that removes silver chloride from the photograph.

6 Twentieth-century black-and-white film had quick light-reacting silver bromide salts. This meant you could take action-photos.

7 Some of these salts were so sensitive to light you could take a photo from Earth of a candle flame on the Moon!

ELECTRIFYING REACTIONS

One incredibly useful type of reaction is electrolysis. It was developed by scientific superstar Michael Faraday.

Hall of fame: Michael Faraday (1791–1867)
Nationality: British

Michael had a tough childhood. His family were so poor that one day he was given a loaf of bread…

He couldn't afford books but he got interested in science after reading books that he was supposed to be binding for a bookseller. He asked Sir Humphry Davy to take him on as an assistant. As luck would have it, Davy was temporarily blinded during a particularly chaotic chemical experiment. So Faraday got the job.

Faraday investigated the process of electrolysis using different chemicals. Basically, you mix compounds with ionic bonds with water and run electricity through the solution. The atoms are pulled towards one or other of the two electrical terminals. The chemical gets torn apart!

Bet you never knew!
One use for electrolysis is in electroplating. You electrolyse a compound containing metal and a thin layer of the metal forms over an object. It's used to make silver-plated jewellery, for example. In 1891 sinister French surgeon, Dr Varlot, used the technique to cover a dead body in metal. The result of this revolting process was to wrap the body in a 1-mm layer of copper. He then put the gruesome object on display. I bet he got a few shocked reactions.

QUICKER AND SLOWER REACTIONS

Some reactions take a second – but others take millions of years. Luckily for chemists, many reactions are speeded up by heat. This makes atoms move a lot faster so they bump together more often. But you can slow down reactions by cooling. That's why food (and dead bodies) can be kept cold to prevent the reactions that make things go rotten.

Dare you discover … how to stop a reaction using another reaction?

You will need:
An apple cut in half (ask an adult to do this bit)
Some lemon juice.

What you do:

1 Place the two halves cut side up. Sprinkle lemon juice over one of them.

2 After a few minutes the half without the juice is brown. It's a reaction between chemicals in the apple and oxygen in the air. An enzyme in the apple speeds it up.

3 What happens to the half with the lemon juice on it?

a) The apple goes black.
b) The apple stays the same.
c) The apple dissolves.

Answer: b) The acid in the lemon juice stops the enzyme working and slows the reaction.

But acids have their gruesome side too. See the next chapter for the grisly details.

APPALLING ACIDS

They lurk in lemons and vinegar and tea leaves and even car batteries. Some of them have killer molecules that rip apart other nicer chemicals. It's appalling what they can get up to. Can you face the facts. . .?

Chemical chaos fact file

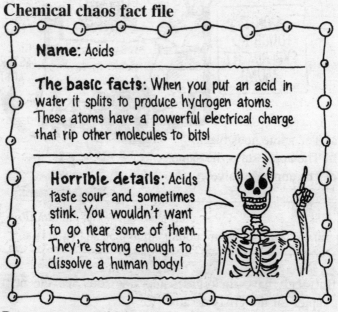

Name: Acids

The basic facts: When you put an acid in water it splits to produce hydrogen atoms. These atoms have a powerful electrical charge that rip other molecules to bits!

Horrible details: Acids taste sour and sometimes stink. You wouldn't want to go near some of them. They're strong enough to dissolve a human body!

But not every acid is quite so appalling. Sometimes they can even be useful…

USEFUL ACID FACTS

1 Amino acids are molecules that join to make proteins. Most of your body is made of proteins.

2 Ascorbic acid is another name for Vitamin C. This useful chemical is found in fresh fruit and prevents the deadly disease, scurvy. The vital vitamin was discovered by two different chemists and they spent the rest of their lives arguing over who was first!

3 Do you like the flavour of orange or lemon juice? Well, that's acid. Yes, citric acid helps make the taste of the juice.

4 Alginic (al-jin-ick) acid is found in seaweed. It's useful for keeping cakes moist and when added to bandages helps to stop bleeding! It's even used in ice cream to stop the ingredients separating. You can amuse your friends by telling them their ice cream started off as seaweed!

5 Salicylic (sallis-sill-ick) acid is used to make aspirin. Yes – the miracle pain-killer is an acid. It was first found in willow bark. People once chewed the wood to reduce fevers. Don't try this – it tastes disgusting.

6 Horribly useful acids were once used to produce leather. These tannic acids from acorns or poisonous hemlock bark killed the germs that made leather rot. The acids are also found in many other substances including tree bark or even a cup of tea, and luckily they don't harm people. But other acids are completely useless.

APPALLING ACID RAIN

What do these places have in common – the Acropolis, Athens, St Paul's Cathedral, London and the Lincoln Memorial, Washington? Give up? They're all being dissolved ... by RAIN! Industry and traffic produce sulphur-dioxide gas. This makes rain more acid. In 1974 rain fell on Scotland that was as acid as lemon juice. That must have left people feeling rather sour.

Volcanoes make the problem worse. In 1982, the volcano El Chichin in Mexico belched out thousands of tonnes of acid gas!

Acid rain eats away at buildings old and new. Even your school is in danger! Oh well, every cloud has a silver lining.

It kills trees by the million.

It does terrible things to fish. They don't grow and the acid dissolves their bones!

Acid rain doesn't dissolve people. But funnily enough, it can turn your hair green. It reacts with copper in water pipes to form copper sulphate, which causes the interesting colour change.

CHAOTIC CHEMICAL EXPRESSIONS

What's their problem?

Answer: No vinegar for their chips.

Dare you discover ... some simple solutions?
Dissolving a bone
You will need:
A stiff bone with no cracks in it. No need to go to too much trouble – a chicken bone will do.
Vinegar

What you do:
Cover the bone in vinegar and leave it for 12 hours.
What do you notice about the bone?

a) It's gone green.

b) It bends easily.

c) It's only half its original size.

Answer: b) The calcium in the bone has been dissolved by the acid.

SOUR SECRETS

You will need:

15 drops of lemon juice

A cup of milk

What you do:

Stir the ingredients together. What happens next?

a) The milk goes pale blue.

b) The milk gives off a disgusting smell.

c) The milk curdles.

Answer: c) The milk curdles because its protein molecules are clumped together by the acid in the lemon juice.

BOTTLED EGG

You will need:

A fresh egg

Some vinegar

A glass

A bottle with a wide neck

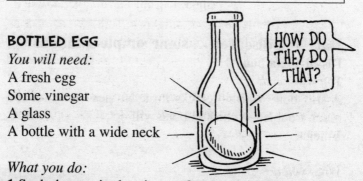

HOW DO THEY DO THAT?

What you do:

1 Soak the egg in the vinegar for two days. The egg will look the same but the shell will be thinner and softer.

2 You can carefully squeeze the egg into a bottle. Ask your friends to guess how you did it.

Bet you never knew!
You've got acid in your stomach. This fact was discovered by William Prout (1785–1850) in 1823. The hydrochloric acid kills germs and dissolves your food. So why doesn't it dissolve people too? Well the funny thing is – sometimes it does – that's when people get ulcers. The slimy stomach wall usually stops this happening but too much acid can cause indigestion.

SINISTER SULPHURIC ACID

It's oily, colourless and turns things to sludge, but it's got nothing to do with school dinners. It's sulphuric acid – a chemical so powerful that it has to be watered down before it can be used safely.

So why bother making sulphuric acid? Well, it does have its uses. For example, you can use it to make fertilizers for plants. If you add acid to paper it becomes see-through. It's often added to toilet paper. Fortunately the acid is washed off later otherwise it could be appallingly uncomfortable. But that's not the only thing sulphuric acid can do…

THE ACID TEST

An acid test is when you use a specially-treated paper called litmus to detect acid. The paper goes red if there's acid around. But in 1949 the acid test was one of lies versus truth and the issue was murder!

In 1949 businessman John Haigh was charged with murder. He had disposed of his victim's body in an appallingly horrible way by dumping it in sulphuric acid. Haigh had boasted to police that there would be nothing left. As he said at the time:

HOW CAN YOU PROVE MURDER IF THERE'S NO BODY?

But Haigh was wrong. The acid had not destroyed the evidence. There were a few grisly tell-tale bits remaining – and a complete set of plastic false teeth. These were promptly identified by the dentist of the murdered woman.

I'D RECOGNIZE THAT GRIN ANYWHERE

Haigh then admitted getting rid of five more bodies using the same method. He went on trial at Lewes Assizes. The jury took 18 minutes to reach their verdict and John Haigh was executed.

APPALLING ACID POISONS

1 Rhubarb leaves contain poisonous oxylic (ox-al-ic) acid. It's there to poison any hungry caterpillar that fancies nibbling it. Luckily, there's less poison in the stalk and it's destroyed when it's stewed..

I'VE SUDDENLY LOST MY APPETITE

2 Bee stings contain acid and that's why they hurt. You can neutralize a bee sting with bicarbonate of soda because this is alkaline.

3 But if you put bicarbonate of soda on a wasp sting it'll hurt more than ever. Wasp-sting poison is a base not an acid! And if you want to know more about bases you'll need some basic base facts.

Chemical chaos fact file

Name: Bases

The basic facts: Bases capture those nasty hydrogen atoms made by acids. So they turn an acid mixture back to normal. You can tell if something's a base because it turns indicator paper blue.

(THEY CAN TURN YOUR FACE BLUE, TOO)

Horrible details: But bases can be nasty too. Some of them have a horrible bitter taste, burn the skin and dissolve things.

Dare you discover … the secret of sherbet?

You will need:

50 g citric acid crystals (You can buy them from a chemist's shop.)

25 g bicarbonate of soda

175 g icing sugar

What you do:

Mix all the ingredients thoroughly.

Try putting a bit in your mouth. What do you notice?

a) The tongue turns purple.

b) The tongue starts to dissolve.

c) You feel a fizzing sensation.

Answer: c) The acid lemon juice and the alkaline bicarbonate of soda react together to produce carbon-dioxide gas. If you add sherbet to a drink you can make it taste fizzy.

SALTY SECRETS

When you mix an acid and a base they react to make ... a salt. A salt isn't simply the stuff you put on your french fries. If you look closely at a salt you'll see an arrangement of tiny shapes. It's a collection of crucial crystals.

IT'S TRUE!

CRUCIAL CRYSTALS

Here's a question to mystify your teacher: What have metals, gems, bones and computer chips got in common?

Answer: They all contain crystals. Some of them are crucially important.

A SMASHING DISCOVERY

In 1781 René-Just Haüy was having a rather chaotic time. He dropped a calcite stone on the floor. It shattered into identically shaped pieces. Intrigued, he smashed the broken bits even more with a hammer. This produced smaller fragments that were still of the same intricate shape. He was looking at crystals!

Chemical chaos fact file

Name: Crystals

The basic facts: Crystals are groups of atoms arranged in little piles of boxes. The boxes fit together to make larger boxes of the same shape.

DON'T LIKE THE SOUND OF THAT

Horrible details: Disease-causing viruses can be made into crystals. The funny thing is, they come alive as soon as they get into a living creature.

LIVING CREATURE

A SICK DISCOVERY

This discovery was made by Wendell M Stanley (1904–1971). He infected some leaves with the tobacco mosaic virus. He mashed up the dried leaves and found that the virus had turned into nasty needle-like crystals.

> *Bet you never knew!*
> *Salt is made up of crystals. If you look at salt through a microscope you'll see them as a pile of little boxes.*

SALTY SECRETS

1 Salt contains the elements sodium and chlorine. Both chemicals are poisonous but strangely a little salt is vital for your health!

2 In the Middle Ages people used to baptize their babies in salt water. It was thought to bring good luck.

3 In France an unpopular tax on salt helped to trigger the French Revolution and the execution of thousands of people.

4 Salt is a major problem in parts of Asia. As swampy land dries out salt is left in the soil and kills the plants.
5 But that's nothing to the Dead Sea. This inland lake is the saltiest place in the world. It's so salty no fish can live there!

CRUCIAL CRYSTALS QUIZ

Crystals can be used for loads of crucial jobs but some of their uses you wouldn't believe. Which of these is too incredible to be true?

1 Diamonds were used to make spacecraft windows for a trip to Venus.

2 Diamonds are used to make lenses for protective goggles.

3 Rubies have been used to make lasers.

4 Crystals are used in some hospitals to kill germs.

5 Scientists are investigating using energy locked up in the atoms of crystals to power space craft.

6 Crystals were used in early radio sets.

Answers: 1 TRUE. The diamonds didn't heat up in the planet's fiery atmosphere. **2 FALSE 3 TRUE.** The atoms in the crystals take in energy and let it out in one intense beam of light. **4** and **5 FALSE 6 TRUE.** The crystals were used to control electrical currents inside the radio.

Bet you never knew!
The colours in gems are due to tiny amounts of other chemicals. For example, a bit of chromium turns a crystal pink. A bit more chromium makes a ruby red. Most diamonds don't contain other chemicals and that's why they're clear.

CRUCIAL DIAMOND FACTS

1 Diamonds are made from carbon atoms. Intense heat and pressure 250 km below ground force the atoms into a cage-like shape.

2 Diamonds are so hard the only thing that cuts them is …

another diamond. Their strength makes diamonds ideal for cutting all kinds of metals. You'll also find diamonds on the end of dentists' drills (that's if you dare look)!

3 The gems are sometimes spat out by volcanoes. This is why diamond mines are dug into volcanic rock.

4 It was Lavoisier who discovered that diamonds are made of carbon. He used a giant magnifying glass that focused the rays of a hot sun onto a diamond. Suddenly it disappeared in a puff of carbon-dioxide gas. The carbon in the gas came from the diamond.

5 Some scientists think that diamonds form inside certain types of stars. If you could find a way to get your hands on them you could become the richest person in the Solar System.

6 Diamonds are so mysterious that it's not surprising that there are many diamond myths. But BEWARE – some diamonds are cursed with deadly misfortune. Here's the sinister story of just one famous gem.

A DEADLY DIAMOND

It was a large blue diamond – unmatched in its beauty and rarity.

No one knew its origin. Some whispered that it was the eye of an Indian goddess – stolen from a temple. And perhaps it was cursed too.

It was sold to the French King and was worn by Queen Marie Antoinette. In 1793 she was executed and her priceless stone was stolen!

In 1830 the gem was sold in a London auction. It was bought by a banker – Henry Hope. But Hope died penniless with his business empire in ruins.

A young Prince bought the diamond for his girlfriend. He later shot her.

A Turkish Sultan bought the stone. A few weeks afterwards he was forced to give up his throne.

A wealthy Greek bought the diamond but he was killed when he drove his car off a cliff.

The next owner was an American millionairess who wore the diamond in a necklace. Her husband went mad and two of her children died in tragic accidents.

The next owner of the necklace wisely gave it to a museum. And that's when the story should have ended.

But in 1962 a museum curator took the diamond to Paris for an exhibition … in his pocket! His plane landed four hours late and the man's car was involved in an accident. The curator wasn't hurt but he never took the stone anywhere again.

Mind you, diamonds can threaten disaster for other reasons too.

A CUT ABOVE THE REST
Premier Diamond Mine, South Africa, 26 January 1905
Frederick Wells couldn't believe his eyes. Embedded in the wall of the freshly dug pit was a prize worth dying for. A huge diamond weighing perhaps

500 grams – that's as big as a man's fist. In a few moments the dazed mine boss was frantically digging out the diamond with his penknife.

It was the largest diamond ever found and it was fit for a king. So the government bought it for $750,000 to give to King Edward VII of Britain as a birthday present.

Now came the tricky bit. The diamond was a rough stone. For its true beauty to shine, the stone had to be split in pieces and each piece carefully cut and polished.

So it was sent to Mr J Asscher – the most famous diamond cutter in Amsterdam. For months Asscher studied the gem trying to guess how it would split. If he was right, the diamonds would be objects of priceless value. But if he was wrong the gem would shatter into fragments. The King would lose everything – but then so would Asscher. His business would be ruined because no one would ever trust him with their diamonds again. He would be a laughing stock and a famous failure.

With shaking hands Asscher set the gem against a wedge. He made a tiny notch in what he hoped was the right spot. He took a chisel and slowly and painstakingly placed it at the precise angle in the notch. His mouth was dry and there were tiny beads of sweat running down his forehead. His hand trembled violently as he picked up a mallet. This was the moment of truth...

Would the diamond shatter? Would it split to perfection? Asscher would never forget the next few moments...

He hit the chisel with all his strength.

The steel chisel shattered.

The diamond was too hard.

Asscher was led away to hospital. He was laughing like a madman and his nerves were shattered – even if the diamond wasn't.

Meanwhile, just thinking about the priceless gem made his skin crawl. But he was determined to try again.

After weeks of treatment Asscher felt well enough to return to work. At last the dreaded day dawned. This time a doctor was on hand to provide first aid.

Asscher closed his eyes and clenched his teeth. He gripped the chisel in one sweaty hand.

Then he struck…

The diamond split cleanly in just the right place. But Asscher was lying on the floor. He had fainted!

The Cullinan diamond was cut into 105 beautifully polished diamonds – each one worth millions of pounds. Two of these are in the English crown jewels. The finest and largest diamond is the Star of Africa which holds pride of place in the royal sceptre.

DIY DIAMONDS

Not surprisingly, many chemists have tried to make their own diamonds. But chaos often ensued. For example, Scotsman J B Hannay blew up his laboratory in 1880 after heating carbon in an iron tube.

Henri Moissan, the discoverer of fluoride, knew that diamonds are sometimes found in meteorites. So he decided to make his own shooting star. He melted a lump of iron with carbon in the middle. But he didn't find any diamonds.

Eventually, scientists learnt how to make diamonds. You've got to heat graphite to 1,500°C (2,732°F) under massive pressure. Thousands of tiny crystals appear. But it takes a week of this treatment to make even a small diamond.

Dare you discover ... how to make your own crystals?

You will need:

A beaker

Salt and warm water

Food colour

What you do:

1 Mix the salt and water in the beaker so that the salt dissolves.

2 Add the food colour.

3 Leave the mixture in a warm, sunny place for about two days. Sit back and wait for a reaction.

So what happens?

a) You return to find priceless gems have formed in your beaker.

THE ANSWER'S CRYSTAL CLEAR TO ME NOW

b) The mixture evaporates down and coloured crystals appear.

c) You can fish some shiny lumps out of the beaker with a spoon.

Bet you never knew!

Buckminsterfullerene is the name given to a form of carbon discovered in 1985. It forms hollow crystals in the shape of footballs. They're named after Richard Buckminster Fuller (1895–1983) an American architect who designed domes of this shape for factories and exhibition buildings. Buckminsterfullerene is a bit of a mouthful, so scientists call the shapes "bucky balls" for short. They sound very rare and exotic – but they're not. You'll find them in boring old soot.

Mind you – there's a lot of soot wafting about in the next chapter. It's made by combustion (that's the posh word for burning) and fiery explosions!

I KNOW

BANGS AND BURNING

Burning and explosions are nothing out of the ordinary. They're just chemical reactions that get … a bit out of hand. For centuries people have found bangs and burning useful. Read on for an explosive story.

A BURNING ISSUE

Thousands of years ago one of your ancestors made the greatest discovery of all. Fire. Without it school dinners would be even worse – just raw veg and very tough meat. There'd be no heat and no electricity because this form of power depends on burning coal or oil. There'd be no metals because there would be no metal smelting (apart from gold, that is!). And your school would be built of mud because without fire you can't make bricks and glass.

Chemical chaos fact file

Name: Burning/Combustion

The basic facts: Burning is a reaction in which oxygen combines with the chemicals in the substance to make heat and light.

Horrible details: The human body can burn to ashes – but it takes a huge heat hundreds of degrees centigrade.

NO PROBLEM!

CHAOTIC CHEMICAL EXPRESSIONS

YOUR FACIAL HAIR IS UNDERGOING A LUMINOUS EXOTHERMIC GASEOUS REACTION

WHAT'S UP?

Answer: His beard's on fire.

Bet you never knew!
1 Fire sucks in air to make light and heat.
2 A flame gives off heat and light energy. The yellow bit of a candle flame consists of unburned carbon from the candle.
3 Gas can burn with a clear flame if there's enough oxygen to burn all the gas. There are no messy bits of leftover carbon.

Dare you discover ... lemon's burning secret?

You will need:
Half a lemon
A cup
Paper
An empty fountain pen

What you do:
1 Squeeze the lemon juice into the cup.
2 Wash and dry the pen nib.

3 Dip the pen in the lemon juice and write a few words on the paper.

4 Hold the paper in front of a warm radiator. The writing appears on the page. Why?

a) The heat makes the paper whiter so you can see the writing.

b) The heat makes the paper darker so that the writing shows up.

c) The heat makes the lemon juice darker so you can see it.

Answer: c) Lemon juice burns at a lower temperature than paper. This fact is very useful for sending your own secret messages.

FEARSOME PHOSPHOROUS

One chemical that burns easily is phosphorous. For centuries doctors prescribed this poisonous chemical as a medicine. The doctors thought that it must be good for you because it glows in the dark! Then an inventor discovered phosphorous matches.

HORRIBLE SCIENCE HEALTH WARNING

Matches are useful for starting fires. Luckily, none of the experiments in this book involves burning down your school. So to avoid scenes of chaos and other dire consequences leave the matches safely in their box.

STRIKE A LIGHT

In 1826 John Walker, a chemist from Stockton-on-Tees, England was stirring potassium carbonate and antimony with a stick. When he scraped the stick on a stone floor to get rid of the chemical blob on its end, the stick caught fire. John Walker had met his match.

John decided to sell his new inventions and strike it rich. At that time people carried tinder boxes containing flint and steel to make sparks and a bit of dried fungus to burn. Now everyone had money to burn on the new matches!

But the new matches were deadly. If the air got warm and moist, the matches burst into flames. They sometimes set fire to people's pockets and made poisonous fumes. A few customers got more than their fingers burnt.

And there was an even more terrible price to pay. Phosphorous slowly poisoned the girls who made matches. Entering the body through rotten teeth it caused a ghastly bone disease nicknamed "phossy jaw".

When these facts came to light social reformers campaigned to ban the matches. In 1888 the workers went on strike (that means not working, not striking matches, silly). But people didn't stop using the matches until they were banned in 1912.

Nowadays we use "safety matches". They were developed as early as the 1840s. Basically you've got two reactive chemicals – potassium chlorate on the match head and red phosphorous on the striking surface. Since the chemicals don't mix until the match is struck they should be safe enough. But early matches had a mix of potassium chlorate and another dangerous chemical, and they had an embarrassing habit of exploding all by themselves.

Nowadays in Britain alone people use one hundred billion matches every year! That's enough wood for 70,000 trees.

MAD MACHINES - THE SELF-IGNITING MATCH

Here's a marvellous match-saving (and tree-saving) invention. A nineteenth-century French scientist made this bell-shaped box.

AH OUI!

MATCH PULLS OUT FROM TOP OF BELL

As you pull out the match, a spark sets fire to the chemical inside the box. Return the match to its hole and the flame goes out. Brilliant!

JUST WATCH WHERE YOU USE IT!

Chemical chaos fact file

Name: Explosions

The basic facts: Explosions are just a type of burning.
1. "Low" explosives produce rapid burning and lots of gas. The gas blasts outwards causing the explosion.
2. "High" explosives use chemical reactions to do this faster.

KABOOM

Horrible details:
Explosives blow people up. Oddly enough though, most explosion injuries are caused by flying objects rather than the blast itself!

> **Bet you never knew!**
> Methane gas caused explosions in coal mines.
> Miners used candles to see in the dark but this
> led to disasters that claimed hundreds of victims.
> These explosions are rare now – thanks to our old
> friend Sir Humphry Davy.

Hall of fame: Sir Humphry Davy (1778–1829)

Nationality: British

Sir Humphry on schooling…

I'm glad I wasn't worked too hard. It gave me more time to think for myself.

Now let that be a lesson to teachers everywhere. In fact, Davy taught himself science and he must have done a good job. Within five years of reading his first chemistry book he was a Professor of Chemistry at the Royal Institution!

In 1815 he went to Newcastle to investigate the problem of explosions in coal mines. After studying samples of the gas, he found that the explosions were caused by the intense heat of the flame. So he designed a lamp:

GAUZE TAKES IN HEAT AND STOPS THE GAS EXPLODING

STRONG GLASS PROTECTS FLAME FROM GAS

But as mines were getting safer, a soldier's life was getting more dangerous.

A POTTED HISTORY OF GUNPOWDER

1 A seventh-century Chinese alchemist described how to make gunpowder from sulphur, saltpetre and charcoal.

2 Saltpetre is found in rotting pig manure. Early gunpowder makers boiled the disgusting mess and then cooled it to make saltpetre crystals.

3 Licking the mixture checked the crystals for unwanted salt. Eurk!

4 For six centuries the Chinese guarded their secret. Then Europeans somehow managed to steal the recipe and invented cannon.

And muskets that could fire through armour…

And bombs to put under city walls…

5 Wars would never be the same again. The problem with gunpowder was that it filled battlefields with thick smoke. So you couldn't see anything…

6 Nowadays gunpowder is found in fireworks and a similar chemical is used to preserve tinned meat.

IT'S LOVELY GEORGE, WHAT IS IT?

A FIREWORK OF COURSE

Bet you never knew!
One type of explosive was invented after another bit of chemical chaos. Christian Schönbein (1799–1868) was experimenting in his kitchen when he spilt a mixture of nitric and sulphuric acid. So he snatched his wife's apron to mop it up. Keen to avoid an explosive situation with his wife the chaotic chemist left the apron to dry. It dried ... and exploded! Schönbein had discovered nitro-cellulose – the world's first exploding fabric.

BANGS AND BLASTS!

1 The bang in your Christmas cracker is caused by mercuric fulminate. In 1800, its discoverer was injured during a lecture as he tried to show it off. Luckily, you only get a tiny bit in a cracker or your party would go with a very loud bang!

2 Another explosive is TNT – otherwise known as trinitrotoluene (try-nite-tro-toll-you-lene). One TNT molecule will produce a blast one thousand times its size. It just takes a little shock to set it off. Mind you – a blast like that will give you more than a little shock.

3 Amazingly, one kilogram of butter stores as much energy in the bonds between its atoms as the same quantity of TNT! But butter tastes nicer on toast and it doesn't blow up either.

THE MAN WHO MADE A BOMB

Dynamite was discovered by Swedish inventor Alfred Nobel. The blasting power comes from nitroglycerine which is an oily mix of glycerine and acids used by Schönbein. Although he became one of the world's richest men, Alfred Nobel wasn't a bundle of laughs. He was tormented by a guilty conscience. Here's what his diary might have looked like.

1865

Dear Diary

It's *all* got out of hand. Explosives are fantastic and fascinating and fun, and I've never been afraid of them . . . but today I've discovered just how dangerous, dreadful . . . and deadly they can be. There was this explosion in the factory.

All my work's destroyed. And, most terrible of all, my brother is dead. That's what explosives really do. They kill people. It's horrible. And now I'll never see my brother or speak to him again.

149

I'll never touch explosives again, either!
If only Dad hadn't got me started, what
with his underwater mines, I'd never
have thought about playing around with
that nasty nitroglycerine stuff.

No, that's it, finished. No more
loud bangs for me, not even so
much as a pop. I'm going to
forget all about the amazing effects
of playing with chemicals, loud bangs,
fireworks, sparks flying . . . It's just too
dangerous. But it's so fascinating, too,
maybe I could just play around a little,
from time to time. I could try and do
something good with explosives. Maybe I
could invent one that didn't do anyone
any harm. I could invent a safe explosive.
Yes, that's it, that's what I'll do!

∽1866∾

I'm brilliant! I've cracked it. I've invented
a safe explosive that will definitely make
the world a better place. They'll use it in
mines and, well, anywhere, really. And
the brilliant thing about it is that it
won't blow up if you accidentally drop it.
It's so simple to make. I just mixed
that nasty nitroglycerine with
kieselguhr (made from the ground-up

skeletons of tiny sea creatures). That was all! The kieselguhr absorbs the chemicals in the nitroglycerine. Then you fire an explosive cap to set it all off. I'm going to call my new invention - "dynamite".

~1895~

Disaster! My wonderful life-saving invention has gone horribly wrong. It's out of control. It's made me rich beyond my wildest dreams, but what good is the money when they use my invention for weapons of war? I wish I'd never discovered it. I want to be remembered for good deeds, not bad.

But if I can't get it right, maybe someone else can. I'm going to use my fortune to fund a really special prize. It will be presented every year, and given to people whose inventions do truly great things for science, the arts . . . and peace. That should make the world a better place . . . shouldn't it?

But can chemicals really make the world a better place?

151

CHEMICAL CHAOS?

Chemicals cause chaos – if we don't look after them properly, if they explode at the wrong moment, or if we let them loose without knowing what they'll do to the environment. So are we cooking up a chaotic chemical catastrophe? Or is it just the chaos of invention?

As ever, it's always the bad news that hits the headlines first. (You don't hear so much about the exciting new discoveries that happen all the time.)

A DEADLY DISASTER!

11 December 1979
Just before midnight, 106 train wagons of dangerous chemicals jumped the rails in Mississauga, Ontario, Canada.

One wagon contained 90 tonnes of chlorine, 11 others were full of easy-to-burn propane gas. Witnesses report scenes of chaos with massive fires raging out of control. One carriage exploded at once and another was blasted 750 metres away.

A quarter of a million people were forced to flee their homes as the chlorine wagon began leaking deadly fumes. Firefighters on the scene are working round the clock in a desperate bid to plug the leak. Their first attempts have failed to make the area safe. Meanwhile the evacuees wait anxiously for news of when they can return to their homes . . .

Luckily, the first explosion had thrown the chlorine high into the air and away from nearby cities. The locals were not in any danger, but it was days before the experts could confirm the air was safe. Others haven't been so lucky. Although the chemical industry has strict safety standards, horrible accidents can happen. In Bhopal, India, in 1984 2,000 people were killed by a poison gas cloud following an explosion at a chemical factory. And there's more bad news…

A STICKY SITUATION

Imagine crude oil – it began as the rotten bodies of plants and animals squashed under the ground millions of years ago. It's thick, black, sticky and very messy and people risk their lives to get at it. They drill holes in the beds of stormy oceans and venture into barren deserts.

And why? Because oil is horribly useful. You can make it into substances such as petrol to power cars, bitumen to surface roads and the raw ingredients of plastics.

Trouble is – like many chemicals, oil causes chaos when it gets out of human control. Oil spills wipe out wildlife and turn golden sandy beaches into black, slimy wastelands. And car exhausts cause problems too.

HOW'S THIS FOR PROGRESS...?

The 1900s...

Smog made from coal smoke and fog caused pollution in cities. In Britain smoky coal fires were banned in the 1950s.

The 2000s...

Smog made from car exhaust fumes caused pollution in cities. What do you think should be done about it?

THE GOOD NEWS

Although chemistry seems horribly chaotic at times, chemistry is also incredibly creative. The creative ideas of chemists can make most people's wildest dreams look rather tame. Just imagine a spacecraft made from a material that resists temperatures of 10,000°C (18,032°F) without melting.

If your reaction is to say, "What will those science fiction writers think of next?" you'll be amazed to know that this substance already exists. It was invented in 1993. And here are a few more substances that seem too good to be true.

FANTASTIC FACTS

Chemists have invented…

1 A superacid called fluoro-antimonic (flewer-ro-anti-mon-ic) acid, which according to some experts could have ONE HUNDRED TRILLION TIMES the dissolving power of concentrated sulphuric acid. Keep your fingers clear of that!

2 In the 1970s chemists developed a cornstarch-based substance known as Super Slurper. It was so good at mopping up spills that it could soak up hundreds of times its own weight in water.

155

3 A new sweetener that's up to 3,000 times sweeter than sugar. It's called talin and it's made from the fruit of the West African Katemfe plant.

TOO MUCH SUGAR, DEAR?

4 Crystals called zeolites in the shape of tiny sieves that separate individual atoms in a chemical. They're a compound of aluminium, silicon, water and metals.

And there's more good news…
Chemists can actually use their chemical knowledge to tackle the chaos of chemical pollution.

1 Many of the world's cars contain catalytic (cat-a-lit-ic) converters. The metal honeycomb shape is coated with platinum. This traps the nasty chemicals produced by the car's engine and breaks them down into harmless chemicals such as water.

2 Ordinary petrol contains lead – added to stop the car engine making knocking sounds. Unfortunately lead in car exhaust fumes is enough to take your breath away. Don't forget lead is poisonous! So chemists have developed lead-free petrol and you can use it in your catalytic converter.

3 Every year people chuck thousands of tonnes of plastics in deep holes in the ground. What a waste. But in 1993 a factory opened in Britain that turns plastic back into the oils that they were made of originally. So now you can make old plastic into new plastic.

4 You remember that hole in the ozone layer caused by chlorine-based gases? They were used to put the squirting power into aerosol cans. But they've been banned and chemists have developed safer gases to use instead. So now you can spray on deodorant without causing a stink for the environment.

THE CHAOTIC TRUTH

It's not chemicals that cause chaos – it's *humans*. We make chemicals. We store them, we use them – ultimately we are responsible for what they do.

We can use them for good or allow them to cause chaos and destruction. The decision is ours. Here's what one chemist had to say on the subject. Pierre Curie (1859–1906) and his wife Marie (1867–1934) discovered the element radium. Pierre said:

We hardly know what lies in the future. Except that out of the chaos of chemistry will emerge even more amazing and incredible inventions. And the future will be more fantastic and hopefully brighter than ever before. And that's the chaotic truth!

CHEMICAL CHAOS

QUIZ

Now find out if you're a
Chemical Chaos expert!

Chaotic chemical quiz

If you've been paying attention while reading this book, you'll be as clever as those cunning chemists you've met along the way. Take this quick quiz to see just how much you've learnt.

1 What three forms can chemicals come in?
a) Crystal, plasma and steam.
b) Solid, liquid and gas.
c) Fire, air and water.

2 Why is it possible to bend metals?
a) The atoms aren't actually joined together.
b) The atoms are joined together loosely.
c) Most metals have some rubber in them.

3 What is an ionic bond?
a) A bond made of iron.
b) A type of superglue.
c) A bond where electrical force binds atoms together.

4 What is vinegar made from?
a) Wine that has gone sour.
b) Apple juice mixed with yeast.
c) Grape juice and carbon dioxide.

5 Which precious gems are used in lasers?
a) Rubies
b) Pearls
c) Golden nuggets

6 How many chemical elements occur naturally on Earth?
a) None – they are all created artificially in laboratories.
b) More than 1,000
c) 92

7 What is an emulsion?
a) An acid found in seaweed.
b) An alkali found in soap.
c) A combination of chemicals that don't mix properly.

8 What do atoms share in a covalent bond?
a) Protons
b) Electrons
c) Crystals

Answers:
1b; 2a; 3c; 4a; 5a; 6c; 7c; 8b

Amazing elements

Super scientists can tell which element is which by their potty properties, but could you do the same? See if you can identify these crazy chemical elements by their characteristics.

1 This pongy element is vomited by volcanoes when they erupt.

2 This is the most common element in the universe. It can be found everywhere, from enormous oceans to the scalding sun.

3 This element hates air pollution. In fact it goes green at the thought of it...

4 Without this element you wouldn't be able to breathe (but at least there'd be no more horrible science lessons).

5 This explosive element can mix fire with water.

6 This element is the only common metal that is liquid at room temperature. It can be deadly to humans but you might stick some in your mouth if you're not feeling well...

7 This element flows through your veins and is what makes you see red when you cut yourself.

8 This light gaseous element can't be seen or smelt but if you breathe it in you'll have some squeaky symptoms!
9 This ghastly green gas has been used to kill germs – and people.

10 This light but strong element is very useful. You can do everything with it, from assembling aircraft to wrapping up your sarnies!

Answers:

1 Sulphur
2 Hydrogen
3 Copper
4 Oxygen
5 Plutonium (it catches fire when wet)
6 Mercury (it's used in thermometers!)
7 Iron
8 Helium
9 Chlorine
10 Aluminium

Intriguing ingredients

Chemistry isn't just something that occurs in your school laboratory. It's part of your daily life. Can you match the everyday items below to their ingredients?

1 Washing powder
2 Your baby brother
3 Talcum powder
4 Tap water
5 Ice cream
6 Aspirin
7 Salt
8 Orange

a) Magnesium silicate
b) Salicylic acid
c) Sodium and chlorine
d) Enzymes
e) Carbon
f) Ascorbic acid
g) Calcium and magnesium
h) Alginic acid

Answers:
1d; 2e; 3a; 4g; 5h; 6b; 7c; 8f

Luckless Lavoisier and his daring discoveries

Crazy chemist Antoine Lavoisier may have been chopped down in his prime in the fearful French Revolution, but before he lost his head, he did many incredible experiments. Here is a letter he might have written to his wife – can you match the missing words to make sense of his discoveries?

Darling Marie-Anne,

It's official! Your little Tony is truly one of ze most splendid scientists in the world. I have been locked in my lab doing all sorts of amazing experiments and I've made discoveries that will put all those other cocky chemists to shame. Hah! My burning experiments have revealed that (1)_____ contains two gases – (2)_____ and (3)_____. The first of these combines with the substance being burnt! Next I turned my attention to water. And what should I find? The same chemical can be found in it! Only this time it's mixed with (4)_____. Well, my curiosity revealed other fascinating facts. Did you know that ze (5)_____ in ze ring Grandma left you is actually a (6)_____ form of (7)_____? Oui – that rock is just a plain old lump of (8)_____. Am I ze greatest scientist ever, or what?

Got to stop now, ma cherie – some rascally revolutionaries are at the door...

Antoine

a) Diamond
b) Air
c) Crystal
d) Coal
e) Hydrogen
f) Oxygen
g) Carbon
h) Nitrogen

Answers:
1b; 2f; 3h; 4e; 5a; 6c; 7g; 8d

HORRIBLE INDEX

168

burning 123
dissolving 33
ruined 104
scrubbing away at 39
worms under 33
smog 154
snow 73–4
soap 33–5
sodium 96, 109–10
sodium chloride (salt) 110, 125, 127–8, 137–8
sodium hydrogencarbonate (baking powder) 38
solids 71, 75, 77
soot 138
spectroscopes 18
Stanley, Wendell M (American chemist) 127
steam 71
Stine, Charles (American company vice-president) 50, 52
stink bombs 82
stomach acid 121
Strohmeyer, Friedrich (German chemist) 68
substances, secret 19–21
sugar 30–2, 40
sulphur 42, 66, 101, 109–10
sulphur dioxide 118
sulphuric acid 27, 121–2, 148, 155
Super Slurper 155

talcum powder 39
tannins 25
teachers 26, 75
shrinking 54–6
teasing 25
testing 87, 126
very young 62
teeth 39–40, 91
false 90, 122
rotten 143
teflon 42
test tubes 6, 16, 27, 51

thermometers 16, 32, 97
thermos flasks 23
titanium 97
TNT (trinitrotoluene) 148
toffee, terrific 31–2
toilet cleaners 38–9
toilet paper 121
toothpaste 39–40, 91
touchstone 102
tracing paper 42
tripods 50

vinegar 25, 116, 119–21
viruses, vicious 126–7
vitamins 29, 116–17
volcanoes 39, 66, 118, 130
vulcanized rubber 42

Walker, John (British chemist) 142
washing powder, biological 36
weapons 92–6, 104–6, 151
Wells, Horace (American dentist) 89–91
wine 25, 31
Wollaston, William H (British chemist) 97

yeast, yucky 30–1
Yukawa, Hideki (Japanese scientist) 41

zinc oxide 53

171

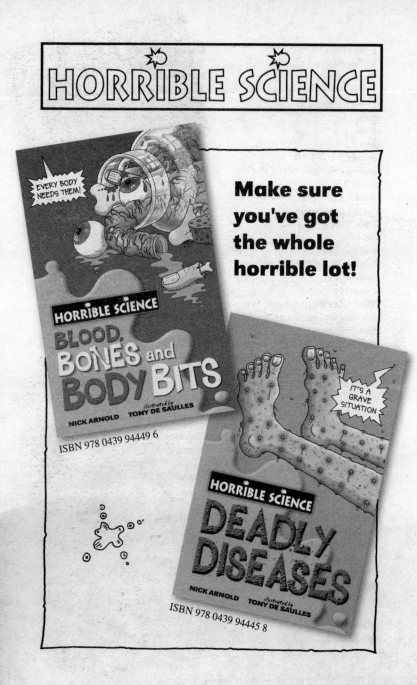

ISBN 978 0439 94451 9

ISBN 978 0439 94445 8

ISBN 978 0439 94452 6

HORRIBLE SCIENCE

Science with the squishy bits left in!

Ugly Bugs • Blood, Bones and Body Bits
Nasty Nature • Chemical Chaos • Fatal Forces
Sounds Dreadful • Evolve or Die • Vicious Veg
Disgusting Digestion • Bulging Brains
Frightening Light • Shocking Electricity
Deadly Diseases • Microscopic Monsters
Killer Energy • The Body Owner's Handbook
The Terrible Truth About Time
Space, Stars and Slimy Aliens • Painful Poison
The Fearsome Fight For Flight • Angry Animals
Measly Medicine • Evil Inventions

Specials
Suffering Scientists
Explosive Experiments
The Awfully Big Quiz Book
Really Rotten Experiments

Horrible Science Handbooks
Freaky Food Experiments
Famously Foul Experiments
Beastly Body Experiments

Colour Books
The Stunning Science of Everything
Dangerous Dinosaurs Jigsaw Book